Elaine Cannon

Putting life in your life story

Deseret Book Company
Salt Lake City, Utah
1977

Library of Congress Cataloging in Publication Data

Cannon, Elaine.
    Putting life in your life story.

    Includes index.
    1. Mormons and mormonism. 2. Diaries—Author-
ship. 3. Biography (as a literary form) I. Title.
BX8638.C36   808'.066'92   77-15451
ISBN 0-87747-679-9

Quotation on Pages 72-73:
Reprinted from *The Spirit of St. Louis,*
by Charles A. Lindbergh,
with the permission of Charles Scribner's Sons.
© 1953 Charles Scribner's Sons.

Quotation on pages 51-52:
From *Letters to Philip,* by Charlie W. Shedd.
© 1968 by Charlie W. Shedd and the Abundance
Foundation.
Reprinted by permission of Doubleday Co., Inc.

Contents

My special appreciation must go to those who
have been the inspiration for my own record keeping and
therefore for this book —
Nephi, Jacob, Helaman, Mormon, Moroni,
and their brethren. Though they are dead,
they live in my heart because I know them
from the records they kept.

And if there were no word about this living, no wonder at the beginning and no understanding at the end, what's it all about?

Yet if there is a record...

The woman was seventy-two when she died. At her funeral someone read the details of her birth recorded in joy by her mother. At the end of her life here was proof and perspective about the beginning, about the reaching and helping and brightening of her seasons. At this dying a kind of resurrection, for the whole family loved their sister and each other anew. A written line or two became their lifeline to the dry farm, the small store mother kept, the loved ones at Christmas or at daily prayer, the father's Sunday ritual, the hard times, the faithful times, the laughing times, and the inevitable struggle to add a new room as yet another baby came.

It was a wonderful, rooted remembering, that funeral. There was no shriveling sadness, but only a hearty gathering of reasons for our being and then moving on.

It seems a testimony in itself for keeping a record of the proceedings of our days.

And here is another.

The teenage son was having trouble relating to his family. His thoughts and his behavior were cluttered with the onslaught of life that came at him as fast as the inches at the end of his legs. His mother's demands especially seemed a burden. He didn't know her anymore. He wasn't sure she understood him at all, and he was shocked to discover that she probably wasn't what he had thought her to be when he was much younger. His older sisters were to him mere replicas of the authority figure he resented in his mother.

Then one day he came upon his mother's journal. It was a temptation he couldn't resist. A perfunctory glance or two, almost a sneer, and then quiet as he turned the pages that revealed a spiritual side to his mother he hadn't appreciated. Soon uncomfortable tears were burning his cheeks. He learned from this irrevocable source that his mother loved him! He also realized that she prayed for him, and that she was mindful of good things he had done. Then he read a note tucked inside, written by one of his sisters for Mother's Day. He'd never suspected that she was capable of such deep feeling. He was interested in reasons she expressed for loving their mother, reasons that simply hadn't occurred to him. The warmth filling his heart opened a door in his mind. He hadn't understood. This record taught valuable lessons at the very time he needed to learn them. He gained new insights in all interfamily relating. He mellowed under the security of such a blessing and of being loved. In return, he felt love for others freshen his soul again.

We who would give our children everything, would even sacrifice our lives for them if need be, must consider the importance of keeping records that can enrich their lives beyond description, and reach them beyond our voice.

Our posterity has a right to know their roots without scrounging for them and perhaps uncovering only part. Keeping records can assure them of this. Writing our life story can help them know their parents. Knowing brings understanding, and understanding strengthens love. And if our own forebears haven't done this, perhaps we can write their history for them.

We should write as fine and complete a record as we can. We should keep current accounts of our lives. We should preserve these and pass them on to the next generation, as we are inspired by the Holy Ghost, with instructions that our children are to add their own histories and records, then pass all the accounts down to the next generation, who are to do the same.

"For whatsoever things were written aforetime were written for our learning, that we through patience and comfort of the scriptures might have hope." (Romans 15:4.) This can be said of the things we write today. We build a kind of sacred supplement to the scriptures as we record our life, our testimony of Christ, our service in the kingdom, our struggles to learn for ourselves right and wrong.

From the land of me to the land of you is one way of describing all personal records: life story, genealogical sheets, diaries, journals, photographic albums, and oral history tapes. What we record in our privacy can be read by posterity, in due time. We then add to their store of spirituality. We train them in the traditions of their fathers. We keep the chain unbroken. So, of course, must they.

We can also find our own way better from our own records. As our behavior surfaces in our writings, lifestyle, frequency of acts, patterns, and problems, we have a valuable roadmap of our own directions. This is as helpful to us as it is to our posterity.

Writing in longhand is one suggestion I strongly urge. It may be hard to read and it may even be more difficult for some people to keep records in longhand than in using a typewriter, but journal or diary entries made in one's own handwriting are more interesting. Handwriting is as personal and as revealing as are wrinkles on the face or markings on the palm. Also, reading a spiritual account in the handwriting of the person who experienced it more surely binds the hearts of the children and the fathers.

Each of us needs to ponder in his own heart the truth that his spirit came from God, to whom we will all someday return. Each needs to know God and to share that growing knowledge by writing it down. Posterity will benefit from such entries in a journal.

Each priesthood holder will one day give an accounting of his stewardship before the bar of God. The sisters have assignments that must be answered for as well. If we keep a current record of activities, goals, and progress, of problems, prayers, and solutions, of loved ones and co-workers, of successes and lessons learned, the accounting will be all but done.

Each of us is to exercise the principle of love for all mankind as Christ taught us in precept and by example. Obedience in putting our lives in order and on paper will help us earn the gift of charity toward others, for in record keeping we are serving. In record keeping we are viewing life with greater understanding.

Each of us is to discover why we were born — what our particular mission in life is. A written record clarifies the question. A pattern of our life unfolds before our eyes as we record thoughts, feelings, and growths.

Let us follow the proverbial journalistic form of questions and answers — *who, where, when, why, how* — as an introductory consideration of the matter of records, histories, and how-to-do-it factors for our own book of acts.

Why?

Jesus told us to give heed to his chosen servants (3 Nephi 12:1.) He who hears the prophet hears the word of the Lord. President Spencer W. Kimball has recently reminded us in a conference address in April 1977 to attend to our responsibilities as record keepers and temple workers, and to prepare our personal records, biographies, and genealogies. Such counsel we cannot ignore. Later in this book considerable attention is given to why it is so important to keep records. Histories are helpful both to the writer of them and to those who will read them. They can't be read unless they are written, however.

When?

Now. The sooner the better. Life is quickly passing. We must start where we are and keep a current accounting. That develops the regular habit of thinking and doing record keeping. As soon as possible the past should also be written about.

Where?

Instead of carrying about a personal journal into public places, some people keep 3" x 5" cards in a pocket, briefcase, or purse. In stolen moments, while waiting for appointments, they record items from the past or feelings of the present. These cards are then stored in a metal or fireproof box until they can be permanently entered into a life story or journal. Others make use of the minutes while a spouse is preparing for bed, or set the alarm for fifteen minutes earlier. Another suggestion is to do our recording on Sunday evening. There are four weeks in a month and four areas of priesthood concern so we could use one week for welfare, one for missionary work, and one for personal records.

How?

Use non-acid, high-quality bond paper that won't easily deteriorate. Use repro-black ink or typing ribbon for the final copy. Write simply or colorfully as is our natural style, but with accuracy. It helps some writers to pretend they are talking to someone as they make a journal entry. It is well to avoid current colloquial or idiomatic phrases that might not be understood by future generations or might prove difficult to translate. We must be sure too that our words convey our real meaning. If there is doubt, a wise procedure is to make an additional entry explaining our concern, thus clarifying the meaning. Another caution is not to scratch out or destroy entries! Historians assure us that the human element makes a life story or journal more valuable.

Who?

We will write about God, others, and ourself. Our life story should include an initial statement about our birth, blessing, baptism, ordinations, and endowment. We should also explain where our complete genealogical data may be found. We'll write about friends who are dear, people who have influenced us, neighbors who have been good to us, leaders whom we'd like to emulate, people to whom we've taught the gospel, and, of course, those special ones who make up our extended family circle.

If we keep a record of the proceedings of our days, we will be in wonderful company. Brigham Young kept at least four large journals besides all else he wrote. Wilford Woodruff kept a daily journal for thirty-five years. Parley P. Pratt recorded his feelings and appropriate details of every ordinance he participated in. Eliza R. Snow's personal journals are fascinating and inspiring. George Q. Cannon kept three concurrent journals that covered personal matters, spiritual matters, and church matters. Joseph Smith kept a journal to record all things that came under his "observation." President Spencer W. Kimball is a record keeper, as we point out with examples elsewhere in this book.

Whether we are their blood relatives, their descendants or not, all of us have in some way benefited from the personal writings and life stories of these people and others like them. While we may quail at the thought of comparing ourselves to such great leaders, our writings and life story can be a blessing to our own posterity and even to other gentle ones searching for help.

Mark Van Doren once said something that seems applicable to the person who would live a full life and make meaningful record of it: "There is one thing we can do and the happiest people are those who do it to the limit of their ability. We can be completely present. We can be all there. We can control the tendency of our minds to wander from the situation we are in toward yesterday, toward tomorrow, toward something we have forgotten, toward some other place we are going next. It is hard to do this, but it is harder to understand afterward wherein it was we fell so short. It was where and when we ceased to give our entire attention to the person, the opportunity before us."

6   The sweetest or the most exciting experience becomes even more memorable when all of our wits are about us, when our senses are awakened and our souls suck it in. To be all there — to see, smell, hear, and note the details, and to instruct one's heart and mind to receive the full feeling — is to commit deliberately to memory a cherished moment in life. We do ourselves a superb service. If we write it down, we will marvel one day at where we have been when the seasons have suddenly slipped us to our wintry ending.

The proceedings of our days may not be as grand as those of a prophet's, but they are our days. To our kin they'll be valuable. And who knows, someone may even read from our record at our own funeral.

he one truly important thing that ought to be said about writing one's life story is, do it. President Spencer W. Kimball has a plaque in his office that reads, "Do it!" When David the king turned over the leadership of the kingdom to his son Solomon, he gave him a father's blessing and said, "... be strong and of good courage, and do it...." (1 Chronicles 28:20.) When it comes to writing our own life story, the counsel seems suitable for us also. Do it!

Life is a grand adventure. Taking this view of our one chance at life gives importance to the smallest joy, the simplest lesson, or even a childish trauma. It is enough to have lived, it would seem. But, we may ask, write about me? Jot down my inner feelings? Take time to record my tender moments with loved ones, my sacred times with God? Bravely account my errors, my struggle with true repentance? Spell out my goals and declare my dreams? Share testimony, trials, frustrations, and the details of my friendships on paper? List my comings and goings, my wanderings, as well as my wonderings? Whatever for?

Here are at least a dozen good reasons for writing our life story:

1. *Because the Lord has said to.* He knows his children and what will be good for them and how his own purposes can best be accomplished. He has always told his children to keep records. Adam kept records. (Moses 6:5-6.) Abraham did, too. (Abraham 1:28, 31.) Nephi kept records and was asked to show them to the Savior during his ministry on the American continent. (3 Nephi 23:7.) Joseph Smith received a revelation at Kirtland, Ohio, that the Saints were to keep a history "of all things that transpire in Zion, ... And also their manner of life, their faith, and works...." (D&C 85:1-2.) The Lord has told us through his prophet Spencer W. Kimball that we should keep a record and that even the angels may quote from it in eternity. We are to keep a current account as well as prepare a life history.

2. *Because writing it down gives us perspective, direction.* Just thinking something through to put it on paper helps

clarify it. Dag Hammerskjold, one-time head of the United Nations, wrote a book that he called *Markings*, a title taken from the signs a mountain climber uses to reveal his route. The markings often show that the climber has to go down a bit to climb up, yet each point is a step in progress. Our own book of acts or markings can do this for us.

3. *Because when we record something, we remember more.* Many precious sayings, feelings, a happening itself would be lost from our memory for life if we didn't take time to jot down the details.

We celebrated our wedding anniversary by preparing a written record of our wedding, the ceremony, and the reception. We listed the goals we had set for our life together during those treasured beginning hours. Each child, grown and gone from our home now, received a copy. That was our gift to them, and though they laughed over it, they loved it. Their gift to us was a written report of their memories of our family life. Even those scattered too far to be present in person sent their reports. We were surprised at the kinds of things they remembered.

How can a parent determine when a child is five what she'll remember at twenty-seven? What a foreverness kind of memory a busy bishop/father created for his family when he stole a moment to sit on a stool in the hall so all could hear and serenaded the six to sleep with songs such as "Abdul the Bulbul Ameer" and "Across the Seas an Island's Calling Me." At the time it was simply a way that worked to free a weary mother from the hassle after bedtime prayers and before father hurried to another meeting. Yet every child remembered this family ritual as a highlight of his growing years. As talk flowed, more memories were added to our record, and a family history was born. It isn't that the incidents are unique; it's that they are something once shared together by people who have long loved one another.

4. *Because a life recorded is twice precious – first the experience itself, and then the memory of it full and sweet when we read about it later.* A single written phrase can trigger a whole remembrance. Like Nephi of old, we may not be able to write but the smallest part; but the experience can come flooding back with a brief entry on paper. Loved ones who have passed on will stir again in familiar ways as our hearts open to special times with them. A child who has grown

becomes an infant again in an instant as a humorous happening is read about years later. Whatever the time — a new baby, a struggle, a church call, a trip, a tragedy, an inspirational answer to prayer — the mood, gifts, message, and ramifications of it flood our minds and hearts. We laugh again or weep anew. Either way, life is inevitably richer.

5. *Because everyone's life is history in the making.* Others will know how we lived, what we learned, what we did, how we managed, how we responded to what happened to us. Time also lends its luster to life as we look back. The simple things we live by can prove powerful as others apply them later. Someone has said that the present is understandable only in terms of the past. But with a life recorded, the future is wrapped in hope. No one ever really dies this way. A life is never finished when it can be picked up and lived again in the written word.

Think about it for a moment. For example, remember that great leader Mormon and his record of how he felt at the final destruction. From the top of the Hill Cumorah he beheld ten thousand of his people who had been "hewn down, being led in the front by me." He described Gidgiddonah and his ten thousand fallen, Lamah and his ten thousand fallen, and all the many other leaders and their ten thousand each. All fallen! "And my soul was rent with anguish," wrote Mormon, "because of the slain of my people, and I cried: O ye fair ones, how could ye have departed from the ways of the Lord! O ye fair ones, how could ye have rejected that Jesus, who stood with open arms to receive you! Behold, if ye had not done this, ye would not have fallen. But behold, ye are fallen, and I mourn your loss. O ye fair sons and daughters, ye fathers and mothers, ye husbands and wives, ye fair ones, how is it that ye could have fallen! But behold, ye are gone, and my sorrows cannot bring your return." (Mormon 6:11-20.)

What if Mormon hadn't been obedient to the Lord in keeping a record of the happenings of his people and of his own personal feelings? We would have been denied a vicarious experience in those dramatic last moments with the Nephite civilization. We would have missed an exotic example of the tragedy of disobedience. Our own future can be affected by reading someone else's history. Others can learn from ours.

9

6. *Because there is an inner drive in all of us to be re-membered.* Eliza R. Snow wrote about it this way:

> "For friendship holds a sacred cord,
> That with the fibers of my heart
> Entwines so deep, so close; 'tis hard
> For death's dissecting hand to part.
> I feel the low responses roll
> Like far-off echoes of the night
> And whisper softly through my soul,
> I would not be forgotten quite."

A personal record at least assures us that we won't "be forgotten quite." The reference to our life is ever there in the record.

An uncle from out of town once visited with our family, and a sweet reunion around the dinner table turned into a rich time of remembering. He was the oldest of two living children in his family. His father had left little record of himself when he moved away from the little brood because of divorce. Our nine-year-old son had a keen inner compulsion to learn more about the family genealogy and pressed his uncle for details on his father's life.

"He's long dead," replied the uncle.

"Tell us. Tell us," pleaded the child.

"I don't know anything to tell you," said the uncle.

"Try," said our eager son.

"Can't remember much. Besides, who cares?" mumbled the uncle.

"I do. He was my mother's grandpa," explained the child.

"Well, sometime, maybe I can remember something," replied the uncle, annoyed at the child's persistence.

"Now! Think! Think!" The boy would not be quieted.

"I told you, I can't remember. Anyway, what does it matter?" The uncle considered the matter closed as the boy sat in silence for just a moment. Then the bomb dropped.

"Well, you're an old grandpa. What if your grandchildren didn't remember you when you died?" The point was driven home. It suddenly mattered very much now that a grandfather not be forgotten. So the uncle tried to remember his father of long ago and succeeded amazingly well, to our joy.

7. *Because to live is a privilege.* It is, as the philosopher

said, God's gift to us. Our gift to God is what we do with our life. Knowing this, we feel greater self worth and are motivated to try a little harder. A life that bears inspection is a worthy one. If a record is to be left of the proceedings of our days, we'll want to make them worthwhile. As we obediently write up an adventure or experience, a lesson learned, a hurdle leaped, we feel a surge of fresh appreciation to God for his gift. It is good to be alive. It is satisfying to have lived. Even the most ordinary life seems extraordinary, the stuff movie scripts are made of, when its record at last reveals the copings and yearnings, the setbacks and small triumphs.

Consider the following excerpt from a life story as an example of this:

"I, the only member of The Church of Jesus Christ of Latter-day Saints in my family line, had struggled long for any record of my ancestors. I had a lead on a cemetery in the place my ancestors might have lived before moving west over a hundred years ago. In the aura of great friendship and the mood of sweet nostalgia as the hearts of the children turned to the fathers, my traveling companions helped me embark on a Shelmadine adventure. Shelmadine is a family name.

"We hurried to find the cemetery in the Pennsylvania countryside before dark. We drove to the top of a long slope, green-covered and tree-shaded, and came to a stop in the midst of markers for the dead. There was mood here with a sky clearing from a twilight storm. The clouds, lightened now of their burden, clung to the hill beyond. The hill itself was layered with spring leafing and rich, black ribbon rows a cultivator had made. There were cow families in the valley between, each newborn wigglylegged calf nuzzling its nonchalant mother. The secret to serenity lay in this scene.

"We sat a moment in the quiet, pristine beauty of the place. It was exquisite in its simplicity. Our hearts soon caught the tempo, and we were close at peace for the time.

"Then the genealogy expert in the group detailed our errand and we scattered like siblings among the sandstone shapes, eager to be first to find proof that my roots might have stemmed from here after all. Then we found it! A Shelmadine family marker! We circled it in excitement, jockeying for position, reading and talking at once about the precious information carved into stone. One placed a fresh carnation on the grave. Another took pictures.

"Once the names and dates were copied we moved down the road where the sexton had directed us to an abandoned plot in the hope there would be more of my ancestors.

"Beside a winding country road, with only a rickety, ragged pasture fence to secure the site, was a 200-year-old burial ground. Here the trees had grown huge around the old markers that had become enmeshed in the trunk forever. A single faint flag of the Revolution flapped over a forgotten hero's grave. Smothered under layers of leaves (home now for crawling creatures) were headstones tangled with blooming myrtle and lush ivy. It was a find we were unprepared for, and a silk paisley scarf was happily ruined in the scrubbing process to uncover data that went way back.

"There were cousins, a brother and sister, and two wives named Elizabeth on a single headstone with the close dates of their untimely deaths summing heartbreak for a young husband. There were others. Did they watch nearby and wait anxiously to be discovered? Did they laugh at this frantic band of friends climbing over fallen markers and wild flowers to uncover yet another lost relative? And did they yearn for the day when their eternal place would be secure through temple ordinances?

"There were no living Shelmadines in the area any longer, but there was evidence they'd been there once. A family marker, a private abandoned cemetery, and a white steepled country church still standing on the land Borndt Shelmadine deeded to a Methodist congregation mark the sleepy village of Shelmadine Springs, Pennsylvania. Its founder lies buried on the green hill. But for me and mine he lives again in our hearts after our Shelmadine adventure."

What a wonderful way to remember a precious hour of a lifetime! A written record with details of weather, setting, and mood that the mind might not furnish at a later time is valuable. People who live deeply ought to write about it. It is, after all, such a gift God has granted us, one we'll value more as the record of the marvelous happenings grows.

8. *Because we can learn from ourselves — from where we have been and where not to go again; what worked and what caused*

pain. We gain precious understanding of the plan of life as we watch it unfold or look back on its sum. I once heard Elder Richard L. Evans say he couldn't remember all the books he'd read, but the sum of them was what he was. And I can no more remember all my precious life experiences than all the meals I've eaten, but the sum of them is what I am. Surely there is a pattern to a life, similar to the lives of others who are engaged in the Master's plan, of course, but unique just the same in the details. Writing it down helps us sort out our differences.

13

There is a stirring example for us in Alma's talk to Helaman that he recorded by his own hand. He speaks of being racked with torment in the memory of his sins until he was forgiven by the Lord. How many of us have been encouraged by this account of repentance! There is more here about learning than can be achieved from records. Alma transferred the records to Helaman with instructions that seem to prove the value in record keeping as a teaching tool. He explained that the plates had "enlarged the memory of this people, yea, and convinced many of the error of their ways, and brought them to the knowledge of their God unto the salvation of their souls. Yea, I say unto you, were it not for these things that these records do contain, which are on these plates, Ammon and his brethren could not have convinced so many thousands of the Lamanites of the incorrect tradition of their fathers; yea, these records and their words brought them unto repentance. . . ." (Alma 37:8-9.)

Our records can do this for us and our children. If it were not so, surely the Lord wouldn't have asked us — as well as the Book of Mormon people — to be a record-keeping people.

9. *Because if we don't, who will?* The Lamanites became a barbaric people partly because they had no records to learn the language and traditions of their fathers. We are a covenant people. We must keep records so that our children will have records from which to learn the traditions of their fathers. (See Mosiah 1:2-7.)

A life story is valuable to others. It is a link between the generations. Parents will delight in the life story kept by their child. Children can find the same pleasure in a parent's story. To know mother or father as a person with a childhood and growing pains opens up all kinds of new realms in the relationship.

I wrote a portion of my life during a period of deep trial in our family. I looked back to my young years to bolster my faith, find direction, remember counsel from parents and wise leaders, and escape into more pleasant days. What I learned and from whom became a book published by Deseret Book Company under the title *The Summer of My Content*. The first copy off the press was presented to my mother on her birthday. A few weeks later our missionary in Japan received a copy for his birthday. Naturally, both were responsive. It was a precious gift from me to them. In it they found record of experiences we had shared, of friends we all loved, of familiar places described that held special memories. They also gained some insights into me, their link between the generations.

For example, consider the following excerpts from this book:

"I had a friend who hated summer.

"For me the weeks flew by.

"Mother used to give us a hug and remark, 'The teachers have you all winter. Come summer, you're mine.'

"And what a time we had together. We'd take the open train to the Great Salt Lake to 'refresh safety factors for our environment.' [Environment was a new word then.] That meant being reminded to keep our heads high until we felt ourselves floating like a cork on the buoyant water. It also meant not gulping any salt water and remembering to lick a finger to remove the salt splashed into our eyes before it would burn too much. We'd come home crusted white around our ears, our swim suits stiff, and our toes stuck with brine shrimp, but we loved it.

"In the late afternoon we always got cleaned up, and often we'd walk past Temple Square to the public library. Each time Mother would point out the 'hand' carved by one of our ancestors on the temple. We felt a personal interest in that building very early. Sometimes we cooked pancakes over an open fire in City Creek Canyon because everyone should know how to build a proper campfire, and how to put it out, too. . . ."

"Sometimes in summer my family would picnic under the catalpa trees shading the Capitol's western slopes. We'd look out over the old section of Salt Lake City with its quaint-gabled, adobe brick houses and the beloved black Tabernacle, fat and squat like a potato bug commanding its own place in the shadow of the pristine spires of the Holy House of the Lord (as we then called the temple on Temple Square).

"Mother would tell us stories about her pioneer heritage so we would know we had 'roots' until Daddy, bereft of ancestors who had crossed the plains, brought us back to reality with ambitious plans for the Capitol Hill Improvement League, he being its founder and president."

What parents wouldn't revel in the child's remembering the little things done together to while away a summer in a special way?

Later in the book I wrote about getting my patriarchal blessing and described the deep discussions, the fasting and praying to prepare for this choice experience. "At seventeen I felt very grown up. . . . The night before my appointment with Patriarch Jones I felt a strong need to gather myself together with Heavenly Father. I went quickly out the screened door and stood there for a time listening to the summer of my youth sift by on the night song of the crickets." From this account our son knew the girl side of the woman who had mothered him.

10. *Because a personal record can be a source of important information.* There is always the real possibility that someday, at a needful time known unto the Lord, someone may be moved upon to read a personal record and be strengthened in testimony or assisted in a vital project. The stories are numerous of people whose lives have been changed for the better by coming across a journal in an attic trunk and reading a grandparent's witness of Jesus Christ.

An important historical effort was greatly guided from its inception by a young woman's personal reflections. Clarissa Young Spencer lived with her father, President Brigham Young, in the Beehive House in Salt Lake City. She wrote her reminiscences and even described the room sizes and arrangements, the wall colors and decor, the staircase without visible support, and a doorbell, among other things. When the time came a hundred years later for this structure to be restored, Clarissa's granddaughter, Helen Spencer Williams, brought these records to an initial meeting.

The house had changed considerably since Clarissa lived in it. It was hard to visualize it her way. The stairway was not to be seen. The doorbell was not to be believed. No electricity way back then! But as the weeks of remodeling took the building back to its original walls, her record was found to be accurate. The doorbell was a pull-string outside the front door that threaded through a tiny hole next to the ceiling, along the hall, and out into the back part of the house where it attached to a brass bell. What a boon to the project Clarissa's life story proved to be! Her notes were carefully followed, and the Beehive House on South Temple in downtown Salt Lake City stands today as one of the finest and most authentic restoration projects in America.

But it was more than wall color and mantel arrangements that Clarissa lent the new Beehive House. She had written of family prayers, suppers, famous guests, a father's counsel, the halls ringing with children's laughter one minute and echoing with hymns from the parlor the next. She provided the spirit that the directors and guides strive to maintain today.

One feels this spirit in walking from room to room, up the long stairs, and past the children's "fairy window" in the beautiful pioneer home. The restoration of walls is one thing. The re-creation of a mood is another. Visitors come inside the Beehive House and feel warmed and wholesome. They feel safe, sure the Young family will be right back. And all because of Clarissa's remembrance recorded for posterity. How valuable her link between the generations!

11. *Because God is in the details of our life.* Born of him spiritually, we are obligated to share with others our experiences with him.

President Wilford Woodruff kept a journal and counseled the Saints to keep one as well. He said, "Men should write things down which God has made known to them. Whether things are important or not often depends on God's purposes. But the testimony of the goodness of God and the things he has wrought in the lives of men will always be important."

Sister Mary Curita once painted a colorful poster emblazoned with these wise words: "To believe in God is to know all the rules will be fair and there will be wonderful surprises." All along life's path there are wonderful surprises in life if we put our faith in God. He has asked us to keep a journal, to write our life story, to secure the past for the future, to make our testimonies available to others with the written word. If we have faith, we'll comply and the surprises and blessings will follow.

The surprise can come in the form of a blessing to one of our descendants.

A college girl was in a state of unhappiness in her home relationships. Her parents didn't understand, she thought. Too strict! One day she lashed out at her mother with the familiar cry of youth to age, "I'm my own person. I can make my own decisions. It just doesn't have anything to do with anyone else."

"But it does, my dear," the mother quickly but quietly replied. "Wait here a moment and let me show you something." She hurried out of the room and returned with a battered copy of her great-grandmother's journal kept on the pioneer trek across the plains. The journal keeper had recorded a trying experience of giving birth to a new baby in a wagon bed, of discomfort and fever in raging heat with no water or help. She wrote of wanting to give up and die rather than continue the journey under such circumstances. But she realized that the decision she made would have its effect on those who came after her. So she prayed, clinging to life with a fierce fighting spirit and faith in God. Her decision indeed affected the life of the great-great-granddaughter who read the words generations later.

Then the mother of the young woman shared her own experience. "In my journal I recorded the agonizing decision I had to make between marrying an exciting man I thought I loved but who was not active in the Church, and your father, who was deeply committed to the gospel. I made that decision on the basis of what would be best for my children's lives — for you, darling daughter."

As the young woman told me this story, she confessed that the experience with records and decisions was a turning point in her own life. She realized that her own decisions and behavior did not affect herself alone. She began to change her ways. And she began keeping a personal journal!

A record with God in the details can be a spiritual feast for our own souls. When we count our blessings on paper, our gratitude soars. It's all so evident — God is good to us and we are forever ungrateful servants, as the scriptures suggest. The things of the Lord are known by the Spirit, and even if, like Ammon, we can only declare the smallest part of what we feel, it may be just enough to lift someone else to a higher plane or to awaken our own humility.

There are important precedents for record keeping. Friends and followers, prophets and disciples of Christ have always done so. By commandment. In obedience and with much joy. Adam, Abraham, Paul and Peter, Nephi and Alma, and, of course, Mormon — these are but a few we know who kept records. And because of them and others like them, we are blessed with special collections of records that we know today as scriptures. From them we learn the traditions of our fathers in worshiping God, in disciplining self, in honoring parents, in relating to others, in treasuring family ties, in delighting in life, and in seeking after the kingdom of heaven. By these records we will be judged.

12. *Because the leaders of the Church are encouraging everyone to do so.* It is part of the program. The following statement from a priesthood genealogy article tells why: "The family books of remembrance in Latter-day Saint homes today should rate in importance second only to the standard works. These family records are supplements to the scriptures, aiding in teaching the gospel of Jesus Christ to the posterity of faithful members of the Church. A knowledge of the written testimonies and spiritual experiences of family members and of the proved genealogies of the fathers serves to bind the hearts of the children to their fathers and helps them to understand the doctrines that pertain to the exaltation of the family." (*Improvement Era*, April 1966, pp. 294-95.)

But no good can come to ourselves or to anyone else if there is no record of our own to enrich and enlighten. Indeed, perhaps the one truly important thing to be said about keeping a record is — do it!

The classic example of record keeping is the Book of Mormon. It is our magnificent precedent. We think of the Book of Mormon as scripture declaring the word of God. We value it for the witness it gives us of Christ. But in terms of our finding ways to record our own life happenings, we can look at the Book of Mormon in yet another light, for it is also an amazing record.

I recall listening to a returned missionary bear his testimony of the Book of Mormon and how he came to love it. He said that his mission president, Elder Marion D. Hanks, had challenged the missionaries to read the book in two weeks and to underline in a certain colored ink those portions that had to do with the history of the peoples being written about. The missionaries reported enthusiastically at the end of two weeks. All of them were impressed with the validity of the record. It rang true. The history was indeed a true history!

Then Elder Hanks issued the next instructions. The missionaries were to read the Book of Mormon again in the following two weeks, this time to underline in another color everything that Christ said. What an impact this experience had upon them!

A third challenge faced the missionaries. The next two weeks they were to reread the Book of Mormon, and to use still another color to underline the principles of salvation. At the end of the six weeks the missionaries had read the Book of Mormon through carefully three times.

"We were on fire," the returned elder declared. "We had become immersed in the record. We could now go forth with a firm witness and a new understanding to teach it and testify concerning it. Our efforts had been blessed by the Holy Ghost. We knew the Book of Mormon was true and that Jesus was the Christ."

Recently I tried that experiment myself with another specific purpose in mind. I read it with the sole purpose of considering the details of the record keeping — who kept the records and how they kept them; how they were passed from one generation to another; how the scribes themselves felt about what they were doing; what God has to say about record keeping. It was also a remarkable adventure in coming to know the personalities of the keepers of the records. What a debt I owe them! How satisfying it would be to someday, in some future heavenly site, talk with them about their experiences in fashioning the plates themselves, in determining which of all the portions of life and worship and struggle and joy to write about!

Moroni abridged the Jaredite plates that came into his possession and wrote that the things he read in the records kept by the brother of Jared moved him greatly. He described the brother of Jared as being "mighty in writing" and that "the things which he wrote were mighty . . . unto the overpowering of man to read them." (Ether 12:24.)

This is how the entire Book of Mormon affects me. As I have read it again and again, I have found my answers to life, my motivation for continuing the struggle, my peace in the Savior. But this time I was overpowered by the ramifications of record keeping. What if such records hadn't been faithfully kept by those various peoples? (And without the aid of electric typewriter or even ballpoint pen and tablet of lined paper?) How deprived we would be!

A focused study of the Book of Mormon points up dramatically a recurring theme — that records are to be made, preserved, and passed on to a responsible person in each succeeding generation. The inherited records that make up the Book of Mormon were to be used to teach the children in the language and traditions of their fathers so they would have a full understanding of the cultural and religious beliefs their predecessors lived by. In every case where this was not done, the people dwindled in unbelief very quickly. They became barbarians, unlettered and unrighteous, whether they were Nephites or Lamanites.

The Book of Mormon is an inspirational collection of personal records written by various kinds of people involved in various kinds of activities. It is a selection of writings from the personal records of ancient Americans, spanning a period of about 1,000 years. These record keepers, inspired by God in their writing, now become the source of inspiration for our own record keeping.

There were those who wrote only in the day they turned the record over to their descendant. Others were gifted in writing, and their record keeping reached literary heights.

Some record keepers were detailed in their accounts. Some editorialized on other records. Some were almost bored with the duty of making an account of their days. Some poured out their hearts to future readers, hoping to benefit them. In each section there is a lesson for us as we begin the task of recording our own life story.

As we follow the record keepers from beginning to end, we see interesting precedents for our efforts. What works for one may not work for another, but the Book of Mormon is about people and so is our own life. People have always had the same feelings, faults, and freedoms. But the Book of Mormon is an inspired record and is, therefore, the best possible example for us to follow in our own life story.

Write what we know best

Consider the account of Nephi. In just the first three verses we see something significant about him and about his attitude regarding record keeping:

"I, Nephi, having been born of goodly parents, therefore I was taught somewhat in all the learning of my father; and having seen many afflictions in the course of my days, nevertheless, having been highly favored of the Lord in all my days; yea, having had a great knowledge of the goodness and mysteries of God, therefore I make a record of my proceedings in my days.

"Yea, I make a record in the language of my father, which consists of the learning of the Jews and the language of the Egyptians.

"And I know that the record which I make is true; and I make it with mine own hand; and I make it according to my knowledge." (1 Nephi 1:1-3.)

We know that he had parents who were concerned about him and taught him all the things he should know. We know that he had a close relationship with his Heavenly Father and was blessed by him. And we know that he had suffered. Though the details of his sufferings are not at once revealed to us, the lessons he learned brought him an understanding of the mysteries of heaven and earth. That kind of record keeping grabs the reader right now. Who doesn't want to know about the mysteries of God? We read on. Maybe Nephi will write more of this.

He declares in what language he will keep his journal and that what he says will be true and done by himself.

Now, in applying this example to our own record keeping, we'll want to establish similar goals. We'll want to write in the language we know best. We'll want to keep a truthful account. We'll want to express something about our relationship with our parents and our feelings about God. These things reveal much about the writer to the reader. Nephi was very serious.

"And now I, Nephi, do not give the genealogy of my fathers in this part of my record; neither at any time shall I give it after upon these plates which I am writing; for it is given in the record which has been kept by my father; wherefore, I do not write it in this work.

"Wherefore, the things which are pleasing unto the world I do not write, but the things which are pleasing unto God and unto those who are not of the world.

"Wherefore, I shall give commandment unto my seed, that they shall not occupy these plates with things which are not of worth unto the children of men." (1 Nephi 6:1, 5-6.)

In these verses Nephi explains why he doesn't go into detail regarding his genealogy. The information was elsewhere, perhaps in a kind of book of remembrance or genealogical vault. But he does give a clue that establishes him as one of a chosen family line. He doesn't elaborate on the things of his fathers. Though such details would have made compelling reading, full of adventure and romance, that wasn't his purpose. He chose instead to make a record of the proceedings of his own days and to include things that would please God and His disciples, rather than merely be pleasing to a world seeking adventure.

And he commanded his descendants to do the same.

This is good counsel for us as record keepers. Let us not waste time and space writing about things that are not of worth to the children of men. And let us write of our own life, that which we know best. Then if there is time, perhaps we will write of an ancestor.

Our own attitude about record keeping

The following passage not only can teach us something important about Nephi, but also can stir up in our own minds a kind of entry to put into our own life story:

"And now I, Nephi, cannot write all the things which were taught among my people; neither am I mighty in writing, like unto speaking; for when a man speaketh by the power of the Holy Ghost the power of the Holy Ghost carrieth it unto the hearts of the children of men.

"But behold, there are many that harden their hearts against the Holy Spirit, that it hath no place in them; wherefore, they cast many things away which are written and esteem them as things of naught." (2 Nephi 33:1-2.)

Then Nephi pours out a plea to his readers, whoever they might be, testifying that what he writes is the gospel of Christ, and those who read his words will be judged by the doctrine. Doctrinally this is a most significant chapter. However, for our discussion on record keeping, it is also a beautiful model of what to write and why to keep records. We should develop an attitude about keeping records like that of Nephi. He caught the vision of the value to others of reading the word of God for themselves. He wrote to persuade men to do good, too. He wrote to make them known unto their descendants, and their ancestors, or fathers, known unto them. These are good reasons for us to write, aren't they?

Nephi encouraged his readers to endure. Surely in our personal journals, in our life story there is place for a powerful encouragement to endure. Our most likely readers will be members of our own posterity. They need our encouragement. We want them to endure!

In his account Nephi grieved that there always will be those who will pay no attention to what he wrote. They will simply cast the words away and, as Nephi recorded, "esteem them as things of naught. But I, Nephi, have written what I have written, and I esteem it as of great worth. . . ." (2 Nephi 33:2-3.)

His words reveal his great love for his people. "For I pray for them by day, and mine eyes water my pillow by night, because of them; and I cry unto my God in faith, and I know that he will hear my cry. And I know that the Lord God will consecrate my prayers for the gain of my people. And the words which I have written in weakness will be made strong unto them." (2 Nephi 33:3-4.)

With our knowledge of the goodness of God and his concern for his children, we can rest assured that we will be blessed in our own record keeping as Nephi was, if we'll pray for help.

We'll be blessed for obedience

We needn't feel inadequate for the task or assume that

because we don't have a graduate degree in creative writing, we can't keep a suitable personal record. Nephi admitted a weakness in writing, but he had been commanded to write, and he obeyed. We have been commanded to keep personal records. We should obey.

If each of us obeyed the commandment to write and wrote of the things of God, the things helpful to others — particularly to our loved ones who might inherit our records — how great life would be. Many more could be reached and moved toward exaltation. Touched by our record and witness of sacred things, a beloved reader might then be motivated to study the Book of Mormon, to grow in the knowledge of the gospel of Jesus Christ.

Jacob was a record keeper who picked up where Nephi left off. He explained how he happened to be continuing Nephi's account and what kinds of things he intended to record. Consider these verses in terms of what might be valuable to include in our own life story.

"For behold, it came to pass that fifty and five years had passed away [544 B.C.] from the time that Lehi left Jerusalem; wherefore, Nephi gave me, Jacob, a commandment concerning the small plates, upon which these things are engraven.

"And he gave me, Jacob, a commandment that I should write upon these plates a few of the things which I considered to be most precious; that I should not touch, save it were lightly, concerning the history of this people which are called the people of Nephi.

"For he said that the history of this people should be engraven upon his other plates, and that I should preserve these plates and hand them down unto my seed, from generation to generation.

"And if there were preaching which was sacred, or revelation which was great, or prophesying, that I should engraven the heads of them upon these plates, and touch upon them as much as it were possible, for Christ's sake, and for the sake of our people." (Jacob 1:1-4.)

Jacob wasn't going to concern himself with the details of history. Nor should we, perhaps. The formal history can be kept by historians. But what things do we experience that prove that God lives or are sacred evidence that he cares about his children? What preachings have we heard at conference? What blessings have been poured out upon those we love in time of illness or calling to church service, for example? Where we know of such things, they should be recorded.

Passing on our records

In the following Book of Mormon entry we learn again how the records and the sacred instructions were passed from one generation to another in obedience. Again, shouldn't we follow suit and not only keep a record, but also pass them to our children, teaching them to do the same?

"And I, Jacob, saw that I must soon go down to my grave; wherefore, I said unto my son Enos: Take these plates. And I told him the things which my brother Nephi had commanded me, and he promised obedience unto the commands. And I make an end of my writing upon these plates, which writing has been small; and to the reader I bid farewell, hoping that many of my brethren may read my words. Brethren, adieu." (Jacob 7:27.)

Now we consider records kept by Enos, a generation after Nephi and Jacob. Again we find a lesson for our own record keeping, and for our lives as well. Enos wrote concerning a sacred experience he had when he received a remission of his sins. What a blessing for us to be able to read this personal account of someone who struggled with repentance as we all must. Our own entry in our life story could be beneficial to our readers someday, too.

"Behold, it came to pass that I, Enos, knowing my father that he was a just man — for he taught me in his language, and also in the nurture and admonition of the Lord — and blessed be the name of my God for it —

"And I will tell you of the wrestle which I had before God, before I received a remission of my sins." This he does. Then he writes, "And now behold, this was the desire which I desired of him — that if it should so be, that my people, the Nephites, should fall into transgression, and by any means be destroyed, and the Lamanites should not be destroyed, that the Lord God would preserve a record of my people, the Nephites; even if it so be by the power of his holy arm, that it might be brought forth at some future day unto the Lamanites, that, perhaps, they might be brought unto salvation —

"For at present our strugglings were vain in restoring

them to the true faith. And they swore in their wrath that, if it were possible, they would destroy our records and us, and also all the traditions of our fathers.

"Wherefore, I knowing that the Lord God was able to preserve our records, I cried unto him continually, for he had said unto me: Whatsoever thing ye shall ask in faith, believing that ye shall receive in the name of Christ, ye shall receive it.

"And I had faith, and I did cry unto God that he would preserve the records; and he covenanted with me that he would bring them forth unto the Lamanites in his own due time.

"And I, Enos, knew it would be according to the covenant which he had made; wherefore my soul did rest." (Enos 1-2; 13-17.)

We'll learn more about how to preserve our personal life stories in a later chapter, but Enos impresses us with his strong desire that the Lord would preserve the records so that the people would not dwindle in unbelief. There are conscientious people today who pray for protection over their sacred records — as they would their flocks and their fields according to instructions from the Lord. We can't take out protective insurance to cover the loss of such irreplaceable items as personal histories and genealogical research, but we can take precautions and we can pray over them as Enos did.

The records now were passed to yet another generation away from Nephi. Jarom took over the task. And Jarom was not a Nephi. Neither is each one of us as devoted to the task of record keeping as are some others we know. However, the lesson to be learned here is that though he wrote little, Jarom carried on after his own fashion and passed the plates or records along to his son Omni.

"Now behold, I, Jarom, write a few words according to the commandment of my father, Enos, that our genealogy may be kept.

"And as these plates are small, and as these things are written for the intent of the benefit of our brethren the Lamanites, wherefore, it must needs be that I write a little; but I shall not write the things of my prophesying, nor of my revelations. For what could I write more than my fathers have written? For have not they revealed the plan of salvation? I say unto you, Yea; and this sufficeth me.

"And I, Jarom, do not write more, for the plates are small. But behold, my brethren, ye can go to the other plates of Nephi; for behold, upon them the records of our wars are engraven, according to the writings of the kings, or those which they caused to be written.

27

"And I deliver these plates into the hands of my son Omni, that they may be kept according to the commandments of my fathers." (Jarom 1-2, 14-15.)

The book of Omni has a bit of humor in it. Look at it carefully. The following verses often are passed over in studying the Book of Mormon as scripture. When viewed in terms of helping us how best to put life in our life story, however, they are invaluable. They reveal human nature — ourselves to ourselves. Human beings are human beings, even in the scriptures. In a few verses — not chapters, even, but verses — the records change hands six times!

"Behold, it came to pass that I, Omni, being commanded by my father, Jarom, that I should write somewhat upon these plates, to preserve our genealogy —

"Wherefore, in my days, I would that ye should know that I fought much with the sword to preserve my people, the Nephites, from falling into the hands of their enemies, the Lamanites. But behold, I of myself am a wicked man, and I have not kept the statutes and the commandments of the Lord as I ought to have done.

" . . . and I had kept these plates according to the commandments of my fathers; and I conferred them upon my son Amaron. And I make an end." After three little verses! Now consider the account of Amaron.

"And now I, Amaron, write the things whatsoever I write, which are few, in the book of my father. . . .

"And it came to pass that I did deliver the plates unto my brother Chemish.

"Now I, Chemish, write what few things I write, in the same book with my brother; for behold, I saw the last which he wrote, that he wrote it with his own hand; and he wrote it in the day that he delivered them unto me. And after this manner we keep the records, for it is according to the commandments of our fathers. And I make an end.

"Behold, I, Abinadom, am the son of Chemish. . . .

"And behold, the record of this people is engraven upon plates which is had by the kings, according to the generations; and I know of no revelation save that which has been written, neither prophecy; wherefore, that which is sufficient is written. And I make an end. . . .

"Behold, I, Amaleki, was born in the days of Mosiah; and I have lived to see his death; and Benjamin, his son, reigneth in his stead. . . .

"And it came to pass that I began to be old; and, having no seed, and knowing king Benjamin to be a just man before the Lord, wherefore, I shall deliver up these plates unto him, exhorting all men to come unto God, the Holy One of Israel, and believe in prophesying, and in revelations, and in the ministering of angels. . . .

" . . . And I am about to lie down in my grave; and these plates are full. And I make an end of my speaking." (Omni 1-4, 8-11, 23, 25, 30.)

These entries are fascinating. They can comfort those of us who aren't too keen about keeping a personal record, but they ought to spur our better efforts, too. Omni, for example, admits that he hasn't kept all the commandments of God, but he has kept the one about making some entries in the record and passing it along to the next generation. His example isn't the best, and so his son Amaron doesn't even write as much as did Omni. But again, he does write. This is one commandment both father and son keep. The next record keeper is Chemish. He records that he saw Amaron make his entry the very day he turned the plates over to Chemish. Amaron, too, didn't write much — just a line explaining their manner in record keeping. And Abinadom, son of Chemish, carries on this poor tradition of sparse reporting but adds one highly revealing statement — no new revelations in his day!

From this series of verses and the weaknesses of these generations of record keepers, we learn how *not* to write a life story. But we also learn that keeping an account must be vital indeed, for at least some kind of gesture was made. At least these people identified themselves and their relationships, plus they preserved the records. When Abinadom turned over the records to his son Amaleki, there was an end to poor record keeping, for Amaleki was more diligent.

This ends this portion of the Book of Mormon, the small plates, which contain mostly sacred writings. The secular history was kept on other records and was in possession of the kings, just as there are historical accounts in our day kept in vaults, libraries, and institutions of church or state.

Recording by the spirit

Now we move into the exciting records kept by Mormon. There is so much we can learn from Mormon's style and methods. He wrote his observations of life and also abridged some of the records others had kept. He also editorialized on these in plates. He was a gifted writer and a sensitive person. One comes to know this about Mormon when his entries are read. Again, we aren't discussing these verses for doctrinal content, but for what we can learn about records.

"And now I, Mormon, being about to deliver up the record which I have been making into the hands of my son Moroni, behold I have witnessed almost all the destruction of my people, the Nephites.

"And it is many hundred years after the coming of Christ [about A.D. 385] that I deliver these records into the hands of my son; and it supposeth me that he will witness the entire destruction of my people. But may God grant that he may survive them, that he may write somewhat concerning them, and somewhat concerning Christ, that perhaps some day it may profit them.

"And now, I speak somewhat concerning that which I have written; for after I had made an abridgment from the plates of Nephi, down to the reign of this king Benjamin, of whom Amaleki spake, I searched among the records which had been delivered into my hands, and I found these plates, which contained this small account of the prophets, from Jacob down to the reign of this king Benjamin, and also many of the words of Nephi.

"And the things which are upon these plates pleasing me, because of the prophecies of the coming of Christ; and my fathers knowing that many of them have been fulfilled; yea, and I also know that as many things as have been prophesied concerning us down to this day have been fulfilled, and as many as go beyond this day must surely come to pass —

"Wherefore, I chose these things, to finish my record upon them, which remainder of my record I shall take from the plates of Nephi; and I cannot write the hundredth part of the things of my people.

"But behold, I shall take these plates, which contain

these prophesyings and revelations, and put them with the remainder of my record, for they are choice unto me; and I know they will be choice unto my brethren.

"And I do this for a wise purpose; for thus it whispereth me, according to the workings of the Spirit of the Lord which is in me. And now, I do not know all things; but the Lord knoweth all things which are to come; wherefore, he worketh in me to do according to his will.

"And now I, Mormon, proceed to finish out my record, which I take from the plates of Nephi; and I make it according to the knowledge and the understanding which God has given me.

"Wherefore, it came to pass that after Amaleki had delivered up these plates into the hands of king Benjamin, he took them and put them with the other plates, which contained records which had been handed down by the kings, from generation to generation until the days of king Benjamin.

"And they were handed down from king Benjamin, from generation to generation until they have fallen into my hands. And I, Mormon, pray to God that they may be preserved from this time henceforth. And I know that they will be preserved; for there are great things written upon them, out of which my people and their brethren shall be judged at the great and last day, according to the word of God which is written." (Words of Mormon 1-7, 9-11.)

Mormon is one who writes by listening to the whisperings of the Spirit within him. So should we. We are entitled to the gifts of the Holy Ghost, and we need only to live worthily and seek after them. Those gifts can tell us what to write and help us to remember things important to our posterity that we might have forgotten.

Preserving our own records

We learn here how many records came into Mormon's custody — the records of the kings as well as those of Nephi. All were precious to him and should be to his posterity. Mormon loved the sacred teachings of the Lord. Though he didn't have room to record them in this particular record, he had them elsewhere. Like Mormon, we can protect and preserve our other records — our Church magazines, the printed conference reports, our lesson manuals, and go on recording our life story as well. Our posterity could find value in them, as we see from reading what is written in the book of Mosiah.

"And it came to pass that he [King Benjamin] had three sons. . . . And he caused that they should be taught in all the language of his fathers, that thereby they might become men of understanding; and that they might know concerning the prophecies which had been spoken by the mouths of their fathers, which were delivered by the hand of the Lord.

"And he also taught them concerning the records which were engraven on the plates of brass, saying: My sons, I would that ye should remember that were it not for these plates, which contain these records and these commandments, we must have suffered in ignorance, even at this present time, not knowing the mysteries of God.

"For it were not possible that our father, Lehi, could have remembered all these things, to have taught them to his children, except it were for the help of these plates; for he having been taught in the language of the Egyptians therefore he could read these engravings, and teach them to his children, that thereby they could teach them to their children, and so fulfilling the commandments of God, even down to this present time.

"I say unto you, my sons, were it not for these things, which have been kept and preserved by the hand of God, that we might read and understand of his mysteries, and have his commandments always before our eyes, that even our fathers would have dwindled in unbelief, and we should have been like unto our brethren, the Lamanites, who know nothing concerning these things, or even do not believe them when they are taught them, because of traditions of their fathers, which are not correct.

"O my sons, I would that ye should remember that these sayings are true, and also that these records are true. And behold, also the plates of Nephi, which contain the records and the sayings of our fathers from the time they left Jerusalem until now, and they are true; and we can know of their surety because we have them before our eyes.

"And now, my sons, I would that ye should remember to search them diligently, that ye may profit thereby; and I would that ye should keep the commandments of God, that ye may prosper in the land according to the promises which the Lord made unto our fathers." (Mosiah 1:2-7.)

These passages instruct us in a significant function and value of records. It is pointed out that Lehi wouldn't have remembered everything he should remember to teach his children if he hadn't had records to help him. To have something always before our eyes, easily accessible to study and learn from, is another valuable insight from these verses. We should keep various records, but we also should study them and search them diligently so we can benefit from them unto our own exaltation and so we can also teach our children.

Others will value our records

The following entry in the book of Mosiah indicates how vital records can be. People want to know about their fellowmen. Records give this contact and provide the information. They span the generations and give people roots.

"Now king Mosiah had no one to confer the kingdom upon, for there was not any of his sons who would accept of the kingdom.

"Therefore he took the records which were engraven on the plates of brass, and also the plates of Nephi, and all the things which he had kept and preserved according to the commandments of God, after having translated and caused to be written the records which were on the plates of gold which had been found by the people of Limhi, which were delivered to him by the hand of Limhi;

"And this he did because of the great anxiety of his people; for they were desirous beyond measure to know concerning those people who had been destroyed.

"And now he translated them by the means of those two stones which were fastened into the two rims of a bow.

"Now these things were prepared from the beginning, and were handed down from generation to generation, for the purpose of interpreting languages. . . .

"Now after Mosiah had finished translating these records, behold, it gave an account of the people who were destroyed, from the time that they were destroyed back to the building of the great tower, at the time the Lord confounded the language of the people, and they were scattered abroad upon the face of all the earth, yea, and even from that time back until the creation of Adam.

"Now this account did cause the people of Mosiah to mourn exceedingly, yea, they were filled with sorrow:

nevertheless it gave them much knowledge, in the which they did rejoice.

"And this account shall be written thereafter; for behold, it is expedient that all people should know the things which are written in this account.

33

"And now, as I said unto you, that after king Mosiah had done these things, he took the plates of brass, and all the things which he had kept, and conferred them upon Alma, who was the son of Alma; yea, all the records, and also the interpreters, and conferred them upon him, and commanded him that he should keep and preserve them, and also keep a record of the people, handing them down from one generation to another, even as they had been handed down from the time that Lehi left Jerusalem." (Mosiah 28:10-14, 17-20.)

In this account we learn that people are very interested in what happens to other people. This is another important clue for us in successful journal keeping. We should never assume no one will care what we did, how we lived, or what happened to us. They will. Someone always will. This is proven over and over again in history and in life and is surely evident in this record of Mosiah.

Personal records are sacred

For us today to have these sacred records known as the Book of Mormon is a beautiful blessing. Believers love the scriptures. A nonbeliever has no use for them, but he might read a personal journal. If that journal contained a witness of Christ, a spiritual experience when a prayer was answered, feelings that an ancestor had about the validity of a gospel principle, his heart might be warmed to learn more of the things of God. The Lamanites had no records from their fathers and therefore they were not prepared to receive the word of the Lord when it was preached to them, as this record in Mosiah points out. So we should carefully record our joy in service to God and growth in the gospel.

Mosiah conferred the assignment of record keeping upon Alma, and it is in this section that we learn something else of value to us in our efforts. Alma had returned from trying to teach the word of the Lord to his brethren, the Zoramites, and he had largely failed. Only those few who "were in a state of preparedness" to receive the word were activated. He was grieved over this and worried lest his own family members hadn't been properly taught the gospel. What he did follows:

"Therefore, he caused that his sons should be gathered together, that he might give unto them every one his charge, separately, concerning the things pertaining unto righteousness. And we have an account of his commandments, which he gave unto them according to his own record." (Alma 35:16.)

Note that the scripture says that we have these blessings (comprising chapters 36 through 42 of Alma) and the counsel Alma gave his sons "according to his own record." Surely we should record sacred moments of inspired counseling with our own children. It would be wise to enter in our journal any sound advice given us by a parent, bishop, or friend. Others coming upon this advice that we held sacred or of worth enough to record could benefit from it too. Isn't this what we have done from the magnificent counsel recorded by Alma to his sons Shiblon, Corianton, and Helaman?

Oh, the help in life as well as the help in record keeping that we receive from study of the Book of Mormon! This is a book about record keeping, and the space here is limited just as it was on the plates. So we must stick to the subject and record here items from the Book of Mormon that enlighten us with respect to keeping records. The importance of record keeping is emphasized in word and in deed in the Book of Mormon, our beautiful model. Down through the generations each person given the trust of the record keeping was obedient, no matter what.

In the verses that follow we learn how the records were passed from person to person. It is interesting to note that not always do they go from father to oldest son. Sometimes a brother or a nephew receives the assignment and the materials or plates. Alma gave them to Helaman, who gave them to Shiblon, who gave them to his nephew (another Helaman), because Corianton had gone from the land to the north on a ship. It is in this portion that we learn that some of the things of the record are written on other sheets and sent forth among the children.

"Now behold, all those engravings which were in the possession of Helaman were written and sent forth among the children of men . . . save it were those parts which had been commanded by Alma should not go forth.

"Nevertheless, these things were to be kept sacred, and handed down from one generation to another; therefore, in this year, they had been conferred upon Helaman, before the death of Shiblon." (Alma 63:12-13.)

All of this happened in about 53 B.C., in the thirty-ninth year of the judges. Note that the time is drawing very close to the Savior's birth.

Though each of us won't have the privilege of storing all the records for our family, or the ward, or the state or whatever, we can be diligent in preserving our own records and training up someone who comes after us in the importance of preserving them. We can't do much about what has gone on before us in our own families, but we can do much about what comes after, as these sons of Alma did.

The following part of the Book of Mormon is from Helaman's record. It is interesting because it is one place that reveals something about the commerce, life style, and housing among the people of that day. It is fascinating to know that there were many different kinds of books and records kept by the various Nephites.

"And it came to pass as timber was exceeding scarce in the land northward, they did send forth much by the way of shipping.

"And thus they did enable the people in the land northward that they might build many cities, both of wood and of cement.

"But behold, there are many books and many records of every kind, and they have been kept chiefly by the Nephites.

"And they have been handed down from one generation to another by the Nephites, even until they have fallen into transgression and have been . . . driven forth, and slain, and scattered . . . and mixed with Lamanites until they are no more called the Nephites, becoming wicked, and wild, and ferocious, yea, even becoming Lamanites." (Helaman 3:10-11, 15-16.)

It should occur to us to write a description of our house, our own room arrangement, where we work, and with whom we socialize.

Have you written about an important discovery you made or a judgment you gave and on what grounds, or about laws that were passed when you were serving in the legislature? What about transportation in your life? How do you get around from home to school, from state to state? To do your missionary work or home teaching? These entries can be brief but fascinating to readers in future generations, and they'll be details we'll enjoy recalling ourselves someday.

We should record in truth

Alma wasn't the only one who recorded counsel to his sons. Helaman did too. And before we leave these particular records, we should consider a point worthy for our own pursuit — a statement about our feelings for our ancestors so that those who come after us will continue the chain of belief, affection, and respect.

"Behold, my sons, I desire that ye should remember to keep the commandments of God; and I would that ye should declare unto the people these words. Behold, I have given unto you the names of our first parents who came out of the land of Jerusalem; and this I have done that when you remember your names ye may remember them; and when ye remember them ye may remember their works; and when ye remember their works ye may know how that it is said, and also written, that they were good.

"Therefore, my sons, I would that ye should do that which is good, that it may be said of you, and also written, even as it has been said and written of them." (Helaman 5:6-7.)

"And thus ended the book of Helaman, according to the record of Helaman and his sons." (Helaman 16:25.)

Our personal records can be valuable to our posterity as we record prophecies and note the signs of fulfillment. This is the case in the records comprising 3 Nephi. The signs of Christ's birth began to be noted in the accounts, and in 3 Nephi 2:8 we learn that the Nephites changed their way of reckoning time to conform to Christ's coming. This is interesting information to come upon. Then we read:

"And there had many things transpired which, in the eyes of some, would be great and marvelous; nevertheless, they cannot all be written in this book; yea, this book cannot contain even a hundredth part of what was done among so many people in the space of twenty and five years;

"But behold there are records which do contain all the proceedings of this people; and a shorter but true account was given by Nephi.

"Therefore I have made my record of these things according to the record of Nephi, which was engraven on the plates which were called the plates of Nephi.

"And behold, I do make the record on plates which I have made with mine own hands.

"And behold, I am called Mormon, being called after the land of Mormon, the land in which Alma did establish the church among the people, yea, the first church which was established among them after their transgression.

"Behold, I am a disciple of Jesus Christ, the Son of God. I have been called of him to declare his word among his people, that they might have everlasting life.

"And it hath become expedient that I, according to the will of God, that the prayers of those who have gone hence, who were the holy ones, should be fulfilled according to their faith, should make a record of these things which have been done —

"Yea, a small record of that which hath taken place from the time Lehi left Jerusalem, even down until the present time.

"Therefore I do make my record from the accounts which have been given by those who were before me, until the commencement of my day;

"And then I do make a record of the things which I have seen with mine own eyes.

"And I know the record which I make to be a just and true record; nevertheless there are many things which, according to our language, we are not able to write." (3 Nephi 5:8-18.)

Many good ideas come to us from this section of records in the Book of Mormon. We learn that Mormon abridges other records and includes some of their important parts in his own, and that he makes a record of things he himself has experienced and seen. We learn also that he is committed to keeping a just and true record even though it cannot include but the "smallest part." We learn he makes the plates with his own hands. We learn he was called of God.

Our debt to other record keepers

The greatest teacher of all is, of course, our Savior. We are indebted to the record keepers of the Book of Mormon for the important instruction that the people received from Christ as he filled his ministry on the American continent. We learn that he used or referred to the various records as he taught. He taught the people from the scriptures in

Isaiah and "all the scriptures . . . which they had received."
(3 Nephi 23:6.)

"Therefore give heed to my words; write the things
which I have told you; and according to the time and the
will of the Father they shall go forth unto the Gentiles.

" . . . Behold, other scriptures I would that ye should
write, that ye have not.

"And it came to pass that he said unto Nephi: Bring
forth the record which ye have kept.

"And when Nephi had brought forth the records, and
laid them before him, he cast his eyes upon them and said:

"Verily I say unto you, I commanded my servant
Samuel, the Lamanite, that he should testify unto this
people, that at the day that the Father should glorify his
name in me that there were many saints who should arise
from the dead, and should appear unto many, and should
minister unto them. And he said unto them: Was it not so?

"And his disciples answered him and said: Yea, Lord,
Samuel did prophesy according to thy words, and they
were all fulfilled.

"And Jesus said unto them: How be it that ye have not
written this thing, that many saints did arise and appear
unto many. . . . ?

"And . . . Nephi remembered that this thing had not
been written.

"And it came to pass that Jesus commanded that it
should be written; therefore it was written according as he
commanded." (3 Nephi 23:4, 7-13.)

If the Savior felt strongly that a prophecy concerning his
coming should be added to the record after the fact, surely
we should take this counsel and example and be diligent
ourselves in seeing to it that important events in our own
lives and understanding are recorded in our records. This is
particularly true for those of us who have lived full lives and
haven't kept an account. We are just becoming converted to
the admonition of our prophet to do this. We should be
conscientious in looking back and at last putting in writing
some sacred experiences, church calls, and ordinances and
our feelings about them and any witness we have of divine
intervention or concern. An example of this is the following
interesting entry regarding the three Nephites.

"And now I, Mormon, make an end of speaking concerning these things for a time.

"Behold, I was about to write the names of those who were never to taste of death, but the Lord forbade; therefore I write them not, for they are hid from the world.

"But behold, I have seen them, and they have ministered unto me." (3 Nephi 28:24-26.)

We don't know the names of the three Nephites; we do have a written witness that they exist. We should follow this example and record our spiritual experiences.

To whom we entrust our records

Another item that it would be wise for us to put in our own record keeping is to whom we will entrust our records. What do we want to happen to our personal journals? Who should have custody of them? Again we refer to our model: note the interesting shift of authority described in the magnificent account in 4 Nephi:

"And it came to pass that Nephi, he that kept this last record, (and he kept it upon the plates of Nephi) died, and his son Amos kept it in his stead; and he kept it upon the plates of Nephi also. . . .

"And it came to pass that Amos died also, (and it was an hundred and ninety and four years from the coming of Christ) and his son Amos kept the record in his stead; and he also kept it upon the plates of Nephi; and it was also written in the book of Nephi, which is this book. . . .

"And it came to pass that . . . Amos died; and his brother, Ammaron, did keep the record in his stead.

"And it came to pass that when three hundred and twenty years had passed away, Ammaron, being constrained by the Holy Ghost, did hide up the records which were sacred — yea, even all the sacred records which had been handed down from generation to generation, which were sacred — even until the three hundred and twentieth year from the coming of Christ.

"And he did hide them up into the Lord that they might come again unto the remnant of the house of Jacob according to the prophecies and the promises of the Lord. And thus is the end of the record of Ammaron." (4 Nephi 19, 21, 47-49.)

Note Ammaron's counsel to Mormon with respect to the records as included in the chapters known as the book of Mormon. Perhaps we should think to record what directions we'll give those who are to be guardians of our records. If we put it in writing, there will be less chance of error.

Help children keep records

The following verses give us another good suggestion about records. Mormon records an incident that took place when he was about ten years old that set the pattern of his life. Surely this is a precedent we should follow with our little ones. We talk to them early of the Lord. We begin in their childhood to save for their missions (not "if" you go on a mission, but "when"), and now we would be wise to learn from the Book of Mormon that when a child is impressionable we also teach "You will keep records. Here is the book for you to start with." Consider this story in which Ammaron comes to Mormon with these kinds of instructions.

" . . . about the time [A.D. 321] that Ammaron hid up the records unto the Lord, he came unto me, (I being about ten years of age, and I began to be learned somewhat after the manner of the learning of my people) and Ammaron said unto me: I perceive that thou art a sober child, and art quick to observe;

"Therefore, when ye are about twenty and four years old I would that ye should remember the things that ye have observed concerning this people; and when ye are of that age to go to the land Antum, unto a hill which shall be called Shim; and there have I deposited unto the Lord all the sacred engravings concerning this people." (Mormon 1:2-3.)

This Mormon does. We now have his skillful touch in record keeping. His kind of record keeping should be an inspiration to us all. He was observant. He was devoted to God. And with deep insight he could record and teach the things of God in a way that would reach people. There is a writing device he uses that is something we might consider in our own record keeping. Certain people are directly addressed in the account. (We might say at one point in our account, "Oh my darling children, I pray you will find your satisfactions in life within the bonds of the church . . ."). Mormon does this so that when he gives specific counsel, greater attention will be given to it by those who need it.

Though Mormon did not claim to be a historian as such, he did pass judgment upon those things and people he observed. He often paused in his abridgments to do a bit of editorializing. And note how quietly, humbly, but directly (as though it happened often) he recorded his visit from Jesus. This method of recording is extremely effective. It personalizes the material so that we, the readers, become carried away in time. We feel we are present at that particular scene. When this method of recording is used, it seems to have been prepared especially for the reader. It is more likely to impress him this way and elicit action on his part, too.

"Therefore, I write unto you, Gentiles, and also unto you, house of Israel, when the work shall commence, that ye shall be about to prepare to return to the land of your inheritance;

" . . . therefore I write unto you all. And for this cause I write unto you, that ye may know that ye must all stand before the judgment-seat of Christ, yea, every soul who belongs to the whole human family of Adam; and ye must stand to be judged of your works, whether they be good or evil." (Mormon 3:17, 20.)

Judged according to the records

So, we all have been addressed and counseled wisely. One is sorely tempted to wax eloquent, if possible, on the importance of remembering all the counsel, for we will be judged of our works by it. But record keeping is our concern, and if we don't keep our records as the beloved Book of Mormon advises, we will be judged for this, too.

There comes now a verse in the record, however, that I must comment on. It is a small statement, almost tucked in as a personal lament by Mormon, yet it tugs at my heart and arouses my awareness of the relevancy of inspired ancient records to today's problems. I quote from Mormon 5:2:

"But behold, I was without hope, for I knew the judgments of the Lord which should come upon them; for they repented not of their iniquities, but did struggle for their lives without calling upon that Being who created them."

What a powerful explanation of failure in life is expressed in that thought in Mormon's records! Surely we today struggle for our lives. If in our own records we were to describe some of our struggles and then — unlike the Lamanites and rebellious Nephites — we were to call upon "that Being who created us," it would be strengthening to our descendants to whom our records would come. It is according to God's wisdom for us to do so. The ancient peoples, however, would not listen. They would not read the records and adhere to the word of God, nor call upon them. Mormon now tells what he did with the plates for safekeeping in those terrible times.

42

"And it came to pass that when we had gathered in all our people in one to the land of Cumorah, behold I, Mormon, began to be old; and knowing it to be the last struggle of my people, and having been commanded of the Lord that I should not suffer the records which had been handed down by our fathers, which were sacred, to fall into the hands of the Lamanites, (for the Lamanites would destroy them) therefore I made this record out of the plates of Nephi, and hid up in the hill Cumorah all the records which had been entrusted to me by the hand of the Lord, save it were those few plates which I gave unto my son Moroni." (Mormon 6:6.)

Even imperfect records are worthwhile

Sometimes we worry about keeping a journal because we aren't skilled in grammar or sentence structure. Perhaps we are concerned because the book we write in isn't costly and therefore won't be considered valuable. Again, we can receive guidance from the now-sacred writings of record keepers generations ago — in fact, nearly 2,000 years ago.

"Behold, I, Moroni, do finish the record of my father, Mormon. . . .

"And whoso receiveth this record, and shall not condemn it because of the imperfections which are in it, the same shall know of greater things than these. Behold, I am Moroni; and were it possible, I would make all things known unto you.

"And I am the same who hideth up this record unto the Lord; the plates thereof are of no worth, because of the commandment of the Lord. For he truly saith that no one shall have them to get gain; but the record thereof is of great worth; and whoso shall bring it to light, him will the Lord bless." (Mormon 8:1, 12, 14.)

"And now, behold, we have written this record according to our knowledge, in the characters which are called among us the reformed Egyptian, being handed down and altered by us, according to our manner of speech.

"And if our plates had been sufficiently large we should have written in Hebrew; but the Hebrew hath been altered by us also; and if we could have written in Hebrew, behold, ye would have had no imperfections in our record.

"But the Lord knoweth the things which we have written, and also that none other people knoweth our language; therefore he hath prepared means for the interpretation thereof." (Mormon 9:32-34.)

Besides finishing his father's record, Moroni took on the responsibility of abridging and translating the records kept by the Jaredites many years before. He wrote many sacred things — wrote again what Ether, the original record keeper, had already written. And he sealed them up from public view according to the promptings of the Spirit. (See Ether 4:4.) Here, too, we find example for our life story. Some things are too precious to share. Some things might hurt others. Yet they should be recorded so that at some future date, in the Lord's wisdom, posterity can benefit from them, learn from them, and be inspired or directed by them.

A personal journal containing such private information should indeed be kept under lock and key and away from thoughtless children or prying and unsympathetic eyes. A statement should be made in a personal will concerning the disposition of such sacred things. We know of one General Authority in the early days of the Church who made explicit entries in his journals and whose responsibilities and experiences were such that information concerning them was far-reaching and could be hurtful if it fell into the wrong hands. He willed his journals to be locked in the vault of the First Presidency. Not even members of his family have access to them without special permission from the current senior patriarch of that family.

If we are going to live deeply and write about it, we must take proper precautions to preserve our records in the best way — some seal things up and leave others to be used and read as desired.

Let us emphasize again how important it is to be unselfconscious about one's talent in writing in terms of records. A life story in its very telling reveals the strengths of the writer to the reader. We write that others may come to know us. This is at least one reason. Surely, if we aren't gifted or professional journalists, we should not try to appear so. We shouldn't hire someone else to write our story. Note in the following scriptural references that even some of the great record keepers had second thoughts about their ability to put down on paper what they observed and felt. Yet they impressed us!

"And it is by faith that my fathers have obtained the promise that these things [these records] should come unto their brethren through the Gentiles; therefore the Lord hath commanded me, yea, even Jesus Christ.

"And I said unto him: Lord, the Gentiles will mock at these things, because of our weakness in writing; for Lord thou hast made us mighty in word by faith, but thou hast not made us mighty in writing; for thou hast made all this people that they could speak much, because of the Holy Ghost which thou hast given them;

"And thou hast made us that we could write but little, because of the awkwardness of our hands. Behold, thou hast not made us mighty in writing like unto the brother of Jared, for thou madest him that the things which he wrote were mighty even as thou art, unto the overpowering of man to read them.

"Thou hast also made our words powerful and great, even that we cannot write them; wherefore, when we write we behold our weakness, and stumble because of the placing of our words; and I fear lest the Gentiles shall mock at our words.

"And when I had said this, the Lord spake unto me, saying: Fools mock, but they shall mourn; and my grace is sufficient for the meek, that they shall take no advantage of your weakness. . . .

"And then shall ye know that I have seen Jesus, and that he hath talked with me face to face, and that he told me in plain humility, even as a man telleth another in mine own language, concerning these things;

"And only a few have I written, because of my weakness in writing." (Ether 12:22-26, 39-40.)

We are to keep records because the Lord said so, and for many other reasons we discussed in chapter 2. But if we obey the Lord's commandments, what we write will, with his help, be useful to someone sometime. He will make our weakness become a strength in the proper time and way.

Record expressions of faith

What fascinating things and sweet spiritual truths we can glean from a journal that includes intimate expressions of faith or insight into the things of God. Our hearts can't help but be touched by the following entry:

"Now the last words which are written by Ether are these: Whether the Lord will that I be translated, or that I suffer the will of the Lord in the flesh, it mattereth not, if it so be that I am saved in the kingdom of God. Amen." (Ether 15:34.)

These are Ether's last words. It should occur to us to record the last words said by a loved one before he or she passes away. Some universities present what they call a "Last Lecture Series," where guest speakers reveal what they would say to others if it were their last chance. Wouldn't it be wonderful if we did this in our life story as a final statement of our faith, our strong convictions regarding principles? Moroni does this somewhat as he finishes the Book of Mormon before hiding it in the Hill Cumorah. What a beautiful and dramatic and appropriate finish to this collection of records, this book that has become sacred to us, the Book of Mormon.

"Now I, Moroni, write somewhat as seemeth me good; and I write unto my brethren, the Lamanites. . . .

"And I seal up these records, after I have spoken a few words by way of exhortation unto you. . . .

"Yea, come unto Christ, and be perfected in him, and deny yourselves of all ungodliness; and if ye shall deny yourselves of all ungodliness and love God with all your might, mind and strength, then is his grace sufficient for you, that by his grace ye may be perfect in Christ; and if by the grace of God ye are perfect in Christ, ye can in nowise deny the power of God.

"And now I bid unto all, farewell. I soon go to rest in the paradise of God, until my spirit and body shall again reunite, and I am brought forth triumphant through the air, to meet you before the pleasing bar of the great Jehovah, the Eternal Judge of both quick and dead. Amen." (Moroni 10:1-2, 32, 34.)

This is an inspired book, to be sure, but as we prayerfully make entries in our own personal journals, our writings can be inspired too. We can be responsive to the Spirit so that we record things that will be strengthening, enlightening, and motivating to our readers. We can record lessons we've learned, the tender times of our trials, prophecies we have heard and, perhaps, fulfillment of prophecies we've been taught in the past (temples being built in far-off places, for example), the unfolding of personal growth, our testimony, and actions of others that have touched our hearts. Then others may be moved as well. Perhaps a grandchild down the span of the generations or a stranger who happens upon our record with the help of God will find value in it.

If we want to be used for the benefit of mankind, helping the Lord with his mission of bringing to pass the immortality and eternal life of man, we must put ourselves in a position to be used by him. Keeping a journal and taking caution to preserve it, as God, through his prophets, has commanded us to do, is one way to do this.

e are about to read somebody else's mail. In the pages that follow we'll have an adventure in people's lives through their letters, which can be exquisitely exciting as records. Letters can draw us close to people. They help us recall events, recreate experiences, recognize traits of character in someone who has been but a name on a pedigree chart. We learn of life style and precious traditions. Through letters we may become aware of eternal truth. Correspondence is another kind of record worth keeping — in addition to diaries, logs, journals, personal histories, autobiographies, genealogical sheets, pictures, tributes, sermons, blessings, and articles.

Following is a kind of random selection of items from various types of people representing several generations. It doesn't really matter who they are for our purposes here. We're interested in them because they did make a record of some kind and therefore are an example to us in our efforts to do the same. Our goal, of course, is to keep a worthwhile record, an accurate record of the proceedings of our days.

The foresight and courtesy of some who responded to the promptings of record keeping by saving evidence and expression of their experiences, attitudes, and associations in letter form enrich our lives in the reading. We learn, we feel, we exult, we mourn again with these strangers who are our brothers and sisters. And they are strangers no more.

Perhaps this is one of the most compelling reasons for preserving a record of some kind.

Late in the 1800s a young Norwegian girl was converted to The Church of Jesus Christ of Latter-day Saints and left everything behind to come to America alone. A pioneer town in Utah was a long way from Oslo, so she never returned to her native land, but her letters home were faithfully and secretly saved by a younger brother. He passed them along to his son, who faithfully and secretly saved them for many years, not sure exactly why he was doing so. These people weren't Mormons. But one day the son of the emigrant woman traveled to Norway to visit with remaining relatives. He was an old man by then. Life and heritage were precious to him as the tie in time became more evident to him. His past was vital to his future.

What a thrill it was for him to be given the packet of letters his mother had written over the years until shortly before her death. They were his only written record of her. As he read them he loved her all over again and felt a sharp appreciation for her struggles and courage. Her letters were simple and sparse, but what joy, as well as surprising facts, this record of life brought to her generations of descendants. They have been read and reread as the grandchildren and great-grandchildren search for clues, answers to questions about the births and deaths of so many babies, about divorce and endowments. Here was a start — here at last was some kind of record to work from!

Finally, temple work could at last be accomplished, and many descendants participated in joy. They knew something about the people involved, too. That little Norwegian girl who wrote the letters was my paternal grandmother. The following are excerpts from the letters she wrote:

"Dear Unforgettable Mother,

"We are doing fine; we have enough to eat . . . but we have had quite a bit of illness lately. . . . It is hard for us because we have no family close by to go to. My husband is good to the children, which helps. I feel quite well, except my back is a little weak. I feel sorry for you and your illness, dear mother, and think about you often.

"My dear mother, . . . I send you one dollar, and hope to send you more soon. I know the boys are helping you, and I feel I should help too. . . . My little boy is so sweet, and chubby. He does not look like me that way, because I am skinny.

Love from your daughter Elise"

"Dear Brother,

"My health has not been so good lately. . . . Once I thought I was ready to die. I was afraid, dear brother, especially when I see all my children around me and wonder if they will be given to strangers. . . . Dear Gustave, you were very young when I left, but now you are a grown man and I guess I will not recognize you when I see you. You won't recognize me either. I am older to look at and have lost quite a few teeth. . . . P.S. Did mother speak of me

before she died or ask you to send her regards?
Love from your sister Elise"

About this same period, Robert Louis Stevenson wrote a letter to a friend. He probably hadn't planned on its becoming immortal, so to speak, but it has survived the years as another kind of record from which many people have benefited. It also reveals much about Stevenson. The lines on having a friend who is welcome at all ages of life are often quoted. Here is an excerpt:

"My Dear William Ernest Henley.
"I was to state temperately the beliefs of youth as opposed to the contentions of age; to go over all the field where the two differ, and produce at last a little volume of special pleadings which I might call, without misnomer, Life at Twenty-five. But times kept changing, and I shared in the change. I clung hard to that entrancing age; but, with the best will, no man can be twenty-five for ever. The old, ruddy convictions deserted me, and, along with them, the style that fits their presentation and defence, I saw, and indeed my friends informed me, that the game was up.
"It is good to have been young in youth and, as years go on, to grow older. Many are already old before they are through their teens; but to travel deliberately through one's ages is to get the heart out of a liberal education. Times change, opinions vary to their opposite, and still this world appears a brave gymnasium, full of sea-bathing, and horse exercise, and bracing, manly virtues; and what can be more encouraging than to find the friend who was welcome at one age, still welcome at another? Our affections and beliefs are wiser than we; the best that is in us is better than we can understand; for it is grounded beyond experience, and guides us, blindfold but safe, from one age on to another.
"These papers are like milestones on the wayside of life; and as I look back in memory, there is hardly a stage of that distance but I see you present with advice, reproof, and praise. Meanwhile, many things have changed, you and I among the rest; but I hope that our sympathy, founded on the love of our art, and nourished my mutual assistance, shall survive these little revolutions undimished, and, with God's help, unite us to the end.
Davos Platz, 1881 R.L.S."

We may not be a Stevenson who had great gifts of wisdom and literary style, but we can surely take a lesson from his book. Perhaps we don't see ourselves as avid journal keepers — yet! But we all write letters. If we would take the time to make them meaningful upon whatever subject — and save them — they would have value in protecting the present for the future. The following excerpt made by a missionary from the letters he received over his two years from his mother are an example of valuable letter writing.

"May 16, 1974
"Dear beloved son in whom I am well pleased —

"You are on your way and I am glad! Oh, how we will miss you, but this is the time and the way to be living now. We are grateful for you, for your endearing, unique manner, and for your honoring this call.

"And now, at this most tender of times, we give you our love, our support and prayers. We have tried to help you understand correct principles; now you must govern yourself. Have JOY!

"The first and great commandment is to love the Lord. Keep it! The second is like unto it — Love your fellowmen like everything.

"The Savior was the ultimate example in this. He gave his life in obedience to God and love for man. He gave the sop of friendship to his betrayer. He girded himself with a towel and washed the feet of his servants/disciples. Can we do less in our own requirements?

"I'll be concerned over your health but never your attitude. Thank you for this peace of mind. I love you and thank the Lord for you in our family.

Mother"

Letters can inform, motivate, remind, comfort, or warm the heart, whether from parent to child, as in the following excerpt, or from friend to friend.

"November 1975
"Dear Tony —

"Grandfather is gone, as you know. No more tricks or painfully familiar stories. And no more sweet, sweet affections and strong reminders that Heavenly Father expects certain things of us. I wish I could tell you in detail all of the beauty (amid the trying times) of the past few days. My love for him surfaced in a most satisfying way. *Real* love, out-pouring on him because of his giving me life and a quality of life; because he taught me to love sunsets and springtime, and prayer because I felt Heavenly Father hovering about him; because of his own valiant battle to be spry and alert when he just didn't have it in him; because he always wanted to pray no matter what; because he gave love back. An exchange of love is the greatest gift in life. Loving is exhilarating. Being loved is flattering. An exchange — where love is received and also returned — is God's gift. So I thank Heavenly Father for a loving dad. I pray your goal will be to be such a one. People keep saying there are many kinds of love. I used to smile and agree. But now I know that there is the love that comes from our being Christlike, and we show it in a greater or lesser degree to child, friend, neighbor, apostle, investigator, etc. Coupling and child-bearing are an exquisite benefit when you choose to be partners. But if you don't nurture and protect and grow in Christlikeness toward your partner, much is lost. The same is true for our friends . . . ultimately all mankind.

"I know God loves us all — each one — the same, but can bless us more as we put ourselves in a position to be blessed. I heard someone put it this way: If you make yourself worthy, the Lord will make you capable.

"I pray that these last months will be so saturated with spiritual experiences — miracles — that your life will always be tipped on the scales toward this richness. I want you to come home and be in the world but not of it.

"Help those Japanese people learn and understand that life is eternal . . . and therefore it matters greatly how they learn and live and love, now.

Love and blessings,
Mom"

Parents look for opportunities to share their wisdom with a child. It is good when it is done in love and written down so that the message can be referred to often.

Charlie W. Shedd responded to an elder son's request to write him a letter about being a good husband. One letter became a series. The series became a book, and the book became a household help.

"Dear Phil,

"Do you remember the night you came home from

school and asked, 'Dad, what good is it ever going to do me to remember what Macbeth says to this babe?'

"You will admit it's no ordinary question, and I couldn't think of a single intelligent answer. I'm sorry, because I did come up with some brilliant ones later. But you know how it is. Certain opportunities have only one chance. So I went blank and there went Shakespeare right out of your life.

"It certainly was not that you didn't have what it took to get through senior English. It was that senior English couldn't get through you because nobody could convince you that it mattered. But ham radio did, and was I ever proud the way you put that transmitter kit together in two days and one night! (Straight, I mean, without sleep!) The man at the store said you might 'mess it up permanently' if you did it alone. But you tied right into those two thousand parts and it worked perfectly the first time you turned it on.

"That's how you have always been. You could do just about anything you wanted to do!

"This is why I am especially glad for one thing you said when you asked me to write you. What you said was, 'I want you to send me some letters, on account of I've got a lot to learn about being a good husband.'

"Over the years I have known many of our gender whose attitude was 'If only *she* would change, things would be just dandy!'

"Of course it isn't true that all the troubles will be your fault. Yet this is a fact you can count on: A wife is much more willing to face what is her fault if her husband has shown that he is willing to assume what is his responsibility. So I am glad for your request and the way you put it. If you keep on developing this attitude, it will be a real asset in all your relationships.

"One sure mark of the 'take charge' man worthy of his position is the greatness of soul that can look in the mirror and say 'Here's where we begin!'

Keep humble,
Dad"

What a father!

And we might confidently add, what a son!

Letters between family members become prized possessions. This is particularly true when one records an incident of life that will strengthen faith, teach a mighty principle, or motivate someone to a higher life style. In the following from a valiant grandmother to her grandchildren, note that she tells why she is writing the letter and concludes by urging them to save it until the day when they are grown enough to understand it. She knew her experience could be a helpful one to those she loved, so she took the necessary precautions — as did Nephi and Mormon — to have it preserved. And now, it is a record of value to all who are privileged to read it. What a lesson for everyone!

This following letter may not qualify as a formal life story, but if this were all a person knew of his grandmother, he'd know she was someone very remarkable and loved by the Lord. She is Louise Lake, a friend and example to many.

"My dear Lezlie, Cregg, and Hal:

"It was so great to be with you for those wonderful days in Tahoe.

"This letter will explain to you why I've had to postpone my visit to you for a little while.

"It was last Thursday, Oct. 8th, when at 1 p.m. I decided to adjust the bathroom window. That meant reaching upward to turn a winding handle. Without any hesitation I quickly moved forward in the [wheel] chair. As I reached up to take hold of the window opener I felt I had gone forward more than usual. I didn't react to fear because I thought, 'Oh, I can easily manage to slide back.' But when I attempted to move back in the chair I couldn't. It was futile. But it was easy to slide downward. I had been careless and moved too far forward. The brakes were holding and the chair was locked The last try I made to return to the seat of the chair, I found it was too late and I was sliding down. I fell to the floor. It was too late to do anything about the adjustment of my useless legs. The left leg was automatically twisted in a cramped position. Yes, it was broken. The intense pain almost took my breath. I didn't have enough room to straighten out my body. I made so many different attempts to push myself up again and again to the wheelchair. I couldn't. I was utterly physically helpless. I was confined to this narrow area. I was lying on the floor for at least an hour before my dear friend Blanche McGhie came in and found me. She couldn't lift me alone, but I was very calm and quietly told her to call the police for help. You see, the policemen are my friends. In about five minutes a very nice officer was here to help. With only one strong lift under my arms he had placed me back into the wheelchair.

"The reason I have written this experience in detail to you is to let you know just what took place and particularly what I was thinking about in that hour while I was lying so uncomfortably on the floor. I didn't panic. In fact, my first thoughts were — what a lesson this is! A spirit of peace came over me as I asked myself the question, How would you like to be sick in your spirit and too weak to rise? Imagine how terrified you would be if after death you were paralyzed in your spirit. If you had slipped and fallen from honorable membership in the Church in this life and had not repented, you would be weak and helpless and confined to one area. As you grow older, acquaint yourselves with those areas spoken of in Doctrine and Covenants, section 76.

"I cannot express what terror and anxiety I felt for those children of our Heavenly Father who find great fault with the Church as they slowly slip and fall away from safety. They fall away spiritually from freedom, peace, and the light of the Lord. They find they are weak and helpless to reach upward and rise.

"Instead of misery, I was filled with the spirit of prayer and gratitude. What a joy I felt to know that my physical handicap is so temporary. If I so comply, my spirit will soar so high in the magnificence of freedom and light.

"As you grow in years and learning of life and the gospel, you will more fully understand this illustration your grandmother has written to you.

"Learn what love means. Be kind — to one another and to everyone around. Kindness is the music of the world!

"You are all very precious and loved more dearly by me than words can express. My wishes and prayers for you all are that in life you may attain and realize that which will give you great spiritual strength and stature forever.

Love and Kisses
Your Lou

"P.S. My darling grandchildren, please keep this letter, because as you grow older you will understand it better."

The next letter includes among other things valuable genealogical information and the inscription from a family tombstone that is an important record in itself. The letter writer is Benjamin Franklin. But even if you had never heard of the man, the content of this letter would be fascinating. It should point up another possibility for getting your life story underway. Carefully read the first few sentences for Franklin's purpose in writing his son. Surely the circumstances of a parent's life would be "agreeable" for a child to become familiar with!

"Twyford, at the Bishop
of St. Asaph's, 1771

"Dear Son,
   "I have ever had a pleasure in obtaining any little anecdotes of my ancestors. You may remember the enquiries I made among the remains of my relations when you were with me in England and the journey I undertook for that purpose. Imagining it may be equally agreeable to you to know the circumstances of *my* life — many of which you are yet unacquainted with — and expecting a week's uninterrupted leisure in my present country retirement, I sit down to write them for you. Besides, there are some other inducements that excite me to this undertaking. From the poverty and obscurity in which I was born and in which I passed my earliest years, I have raised myself to a state of affluence and some degree of celebrity in the world. As constant good fortune has accompanied me even to an advanced period of life, my posterity will perhaps be desirous of learning the means, which I employed, and which, thanks to Providence, so well succeeded with me. They may also deem them fit to be imitated, should any of them find themselves in similar circumstances. That good fortune, when I reflected on it, which is frequently the case, has induced me sometimes to say that were it left to my choice, I should have no objection to go over the same life from its beginning to the end, only asking the advantage authors have of correcting in a second edition some faults of the first. So I would also wish to change some incidents of it for others more favourable. Notwithstanding, if this condition were denied, I should still accept the offer.
   "And now I speak of thanking God, I desire with all humility to acknowledge that I owe the mentioned happiness of my past life to his divine providence, which led me to the means I used and gave them success. . . .

"Some notes one of my uncles (who had the same curiosity in collecting family anecdotes) once put into my hands furnished me with several particulars relating to our ancestors. From these notes I learned that they had lived in the same village, Ecton in Northamptonshire, on a freehold of about thirty acres, for at least three hundred years, and how much longer he knew not. Perhaps from the time when the name of Franklin, which before was the name of an order of people, was assumed by them as a surname, when others took surnames all over the kingdom. . . .

"I suppose you may like to know what kind of a man my father was. He had an excellent constitution, was of middle stature, but well set and very strong. He was ingenious, could draw prettily, was skilled a little in music; his voice was sonorous and agreeable, so that when he played Psalm tunes on his violin and sang withal as he sometimes did in an evening after the business of the day was over, it was extremely agreeable to hear. . . . At his table he liked to have, as often as he could, some sensible friend or neighbour to converse with, and always took care to start some ingenious or useful topic for discourse which might tend to improve the minds of his children.

"My mother had likewise an excellent constitution. She suckled all her ten children. I never knew either my father or mother to have any sickness but that of which they died, he at eighty-nine and she at eighty-five years of age. They lie buried together at Boston, where I some years since placed a marble stone over their grave with this inscription:

Josiah Franklin
And Abiah his wife
Lie here interred.
They lived lovingly together in wedlock
Fifty-five years.
Without an estate or any gainful employment,
By constant labour and industry,
With God's blessing,
They maintained a large family
Comfortably;
And brought up thirteen children,
And seven grandchildren
Reputably.
From this instance, Reader,

Be encouraged to diligence in thy calling,
And distrust not Providence.
He was a pious and prudent man,
She a discreet and virtuous woman.
Their youngest son,
In filial regard to their memory,
Places this stone.
J.F. born 1655 — Died 1744 — AEtat. 89.
A.F. born 1667 — Died 1752 — 85."

57

Sometimes the child teaches the parent. When that happens on paper, every care should be taken to preserve it. How can you place a value on a precious document like a tender love note pinned to the pillow with a tracing of a childish hand as an accompanying gift? It's proof he or she loved you once, even if subsequent happenings may make us question it later! It is proof, too, that he or she was young once and innocent, but very giving and wise.

Sometimes childish agonies, secret yearnings, and even some frustrations about family life that a parent has been blind to before are bared in a scribbled note.

"Dear Mother,
"Why did you go away? When will you be back? Things are not happy for me. Lowell won't practice his 2½ talk for Sunday School. Nadine didn't rins her hare good. It sticks. Iam tired. I never want to be a mother. Do you love me?"

"Dearest Mom,
"Can we please stay home on Christmus day. I like to sit by the fire in the living room. I love you."

Neither child was writing for posterity, deliberately. But they did just the same because parents treasured the notes and preserved them for "some day."

Letter writing is another kind of record that can be the teaching aid we need to help our loved ones become interested, loving, valiant, understanding.

Occasions seem to beg for special letters to be written. A birthday, baptism, priesthood ordination, marriage and mission, accident or illness, end-of-the-year summary of one's feelings about life — all are great excuses to correspond. We can, of course, choose to write any time we please just because we love. In the process we fill in the blanks with pertinent materials. In some circles this method might be called brainwashing. In others it is called recording a personal history.

Lawrence Flake sat with his wife during labor and wrote a letter to their unborn child. He has done so with the birth of each child. These documents or records have become favored possessions of the children. Over the years the letters have been read on appropriate birthdays. The feelings of a father for their mother, for the anticipated child, and for the miracle of being a partner with God in creation have given a powerful preciousness to each child's life and perspective.

Mormon thought of this long before we did. He wrote his son Moroni a letter when he received a new church assignment. The congratulations were brief. The accompanying gospel instructions were weighty. Only a portion is reprinted here, but the entire chapters of Moroni 8 and 9 beg our careful perusal. These personal letters were so valuable that they were etched into precious metal and preserved for all posterity. The sacred truths of God are always worth preserving, and when any parent writes to a child about them, the record should be saved and shared with descendants.

"An epistle of my father Mormon, written to me, Moroni; and it was written unto me soon after my calling to the ministry. And on this wise did he write unto me, saying:

"My beloved son, Moroni, I rejoice exceedingly that your Lord Jesus Christ hath been mindful of you, and hath called you to his ministry, and to his holy work.

"I am mindful of you always in my prayers, continually praying unto God the Father in the name of his Holy Child, Jesus, that he, through his infinite goodness and grace, will keep you through the endurance of faith on his name to the end.

"And now, my son, I speak unto you concerning that which grieveth me exceedingly; for it grieveth me that there should disputations rise among you.

"For, if I have learned the truth, there have been disputations among you concerning the baptism of your little children.

"And now, my son, I desire that ye should labor diligently, that this gross error should be removed from among you; for, for this intent I have written this epistle.

"For immediately after I had learned these things of you

I inquired of the Lord concerning the matter. And the word of the Lord came to me by the power of the Holy Ghost, saying:

"Listen to the words of Christ, your Redeemer, your Lord and your God. Behold, I came into the world not to call the righteous but sinners to repentance; the whole need no physician, but they that are sick; wherefore, little children are whole, for they are not capable of committing sin; wherefore the curse of Adam is taken from them in me, that it hath no power over them; and the law of circumcision is done away in me.

"And after this manner did the Holy Ghost manifest the word of God unto me; wherefore, my beloved son, I know that it is solemn mockery before God that ye should baptize little children. . . .

"Behold, my son, I will write unto you again if I go not out soon against the Lamanites. Behold, the pride of this nation, or the people of the Nephites, hath proven their destruction except they should repent.

"Pray for them, my son, that repentance may come unto them. But behold, I fear lest the Spirit hath ceased striving with them; and in this part of the land they are also seeking to put down all power and authority which cometh from God; and they are denying the Holy Ghost.

"And after rejecting so great a knowledge, my son, they must perish soon, unto the fulfilling of the prophecies which were spoken by the prophets, as well as the words of our Savior himself.

"Farewell, my son, until I shall write unto you, or shall meet you again. Amen." (Moroni 8:1-9, 27-30.)

The Second Epistle of John was written to a woman he obviously loved. It has given all the readers down the years an insight into John and into that lady whom others apparently loved too. That's a good lesson for us in itself. But also included in that letter is some sound counsel that applies even in our day about not listening to dissidents. This is a short letter by scriptural standards, yet we would-be record keepers and especially the lazy letter writers among us can take comfort in this. The length of the record does not determine its ultimate worth. A brief note with a single element of truth becomes a family treasure when one of one's kin declares it.

"The elder unto the elect lady and her children, whom I

love in the truth; and not I only, but also all they that have known the truth;

"For the truth's sake, which dwelleth in us, and shall be with us for ever.

"Grace be with you, mercy, and peace, from God the Father, and from the Lord Jesus Christ, the Son of the Father, in truth and love.

"I rejoiced greatly that I found of thy children walking in truth, as we have received a commandment from the Father.

"And now I beseech thee, lady, not as though I wrote a new commandment unto thee, but that which we had from the beginning, that we love one another.

"And this is love, that we walk after his commandments. This is the commandment, That, as ye have heard from the beginning, ye should walk in it. . . .

"If there come any unto you, and bring not this doctrine, receive him not into your house, neither bid him God speed:

"For he that biddeth him God speed is partaker of his evil deeds.

"Having many things to write unto you, I would not write with paper and ink: but I trust to come unto you, and speak face to face, that our joy may be full.

"The children of thy elect sister greet thee. Amen." (2 John 1-6, 10-13.)

Peter wrote epistles. So did Geddianhi, the Lamanite robber chief. So did Helaman to Moroni, telling of the wonderful faith of stripling Ammonites. And Moroni wrote to Pahoran, scolding him for not helping out in the war effort. He wrote things like this: "Can you think to sit upon your throne in a state of thoughtless stupor, while your enemies are spreading the work of death around you? . . . And now, my beloved brethren — for ye ought to be beloved; yea, and ye ought to have stirred yourselves more diligently for the welfare and the freedom of this people. . . ." (Alma 60:7, 10.)

Perhaps we can learn something about our own letter writing from this — as well as finding Book of Mormon characters more believable. Pahoran's patriotic reply proved Moroni was wrong in being so hasty. He just didn't understand the situation. But his letter did do some good.

"I, Pahoran, who am chief governor of this land, do

send these words unto Moroni, the chief captain over the army. Behold, I say unto you, Moroni, that I do not joy in your great afflictions, yea, it grieves my soul.

"But behold, there are those who do joy in your afflictions, yea, insomuch that they have risen up in rebellion against me, . . . and sought to take away the judgment-seat from me that have been the cause of this great iniquity. . . .

"And now, in your epistle you have censured me, but it mattereth not; I am not angry, but do rejoice in the greatness of your heart. I, Pahoran, do not seek for power, save only to retain my judgment-seat that I may preserve the rights and the liberty of my people. My soul standeth fast in that liberty in the which God hath made us free. . . .

"But behold he doth not command us that we shall subject ourselves to our enemies, but that we should put our trust in him, and he will deliver us. . . .

"And now, Moroni, I do joy in receiving your epistle, for I was somewhat worried concerning what we should do, whether it should be just in us to go against our brethren.

"But ye have said, except they repent the Lord hath commanded that ye should go against them.

"See that ye strengthen Lehi and Teancum in the Lord; tell them to fear not, for God will deliver them, yea, and also all those who stand fast in that liberty wherewith God hath made them free. And now I close mine epistle to my beloved brother, Moroni." (Alma 61:2-4, 9, 13, 19-21.)

"And . . . when Moroni had received this epistle his heart did take courage, and was filled with exceeding great joy because of the faithfulness of Pahoran, that he was not also a traitor to the freedom and cause of his country." (Alma 62:1.)

The scriptures are full of letters from one person to another, or from leadership to a congregation. Had these letters not been filed away in safety, a world would have been bereft of some beautiful saving principles. Peter wrote to the Thessalonians exhorting them to be steadfast and not weary in well doing, but he also said, "And if any man obey not our word by this epistle, note that man, and have no company with him, that he may be ashamed. Yet count him not as an enemy, but admonish him as a brother." (2 Thessalonians 3:14-15.) This puts a special value on material that goes out from church leaders to their flock.

When my husband was a young bishop he prepared an Easter message for the ward bulletin. It was on the resurrection. One family hadn't bothered to read it but tossed the bulletin into a desk drawer and promptly forgot it. Many months later the wife died. The father had been inactive in the Church, and had little with which to fortify himself in such a crisis. Then one day he happened on that message from the bulletin. Another kind of record that became a blessing long after it was written! The man now was ready to learn. His expressions of appreciation revealed to us just how needful he'd been and how grateful he was now for written word he could read quietly in a time of need.

There are, as we have said, many kinds of records. Funeral sermons, patriarchal blessings, a family chore chart, inscriptions in a book, clippings, explanatory material taped to the underside of an object of art or souvenir, notes on a desk pad — all are life-style revealing and heart-warming.

On August 19, 1895, Susa Young Gates, Mormon mother of thirteen, Church leader, and enthusiastic member of the International Council of Women, made some notes regarding her activities for the day. Her list included these:

"Go down cellar with Emma and show her how to clean it.

"Darn Dan's stockings.

"Boil over the bottle of spoiled fruit. Write down plan of altering the house which came to me in the night.

"Clean my office.

"Prepare talk on 'Women and Literature' and attend the Academy's opening exercises at 10 o'clock.

"Write article for Young Women's Journal."

Interesting? Of course! Informative and inspiring, too. I hope I'm able to cross paths with Susa Y. Gates in eternity. If this record of one day in her life is any indication, she'll be some special soul to meet.

The list of things to do is another kind of record, to be sure. It gives us an idea of where else to look for information about our loved ones. But how much better if, in addition to the trappings of a life-style, we had a personal history, an autobiography, or some diaries in the handwriting of a loved one?

Children are incredibly responsive to the things of

truth. They are yet so fresh from Heavenly Father. We don't have to coax them to become involved in a project of personal history and preserving evidence of their presence on earth. Even if we didn't start such a family activity when they were little, it still will catch their support if we help them see the adventure and significance and continuity in life.

One family combines teaching the Book of Mormon miracle of the visits of Moroni to Joseph Smith with keeping a family history. Each year on the wedding anniversary of the parents, which is the day the family officially began, there is a special kind of Hill Cumorah ceremony at their house. They get ready for it all year long. During the months each one selects things he'd like to preserve in the box. Their records include tapes made of their achievements — an instrument mastered, a talk given, a baby's first words, a blessing father gave to mother before surgery, a family interview with an important visitor, testimonies expressed. Height, weight, handwriting, and a lock of hair are included too. Some drawings, crafts, or other special treasures are selected; the family picture, an updated history, plus special spiritual instructions from the bishop or the prophet go into the box. When everything is ready there is a family prayer and a review of Moroni-to-Joseph details as the family gathers at a special spot in their backyard. They're taught once more that it is a sacred box to be kept secret from others and the ground is never to be disturbed until the proper time when all are there. No neighborhood diggings, in other words.

Each has a turn with the shovel to uncover the strong box buried in special wrappings the year before. Excitement runs high by now. Little hearts beat as the box is opened, its contents fondly examined, and family progress noted. A year is a century to a child. The remembering and comparing evoke both laughter and soberness.

The new records are added before the box goes back into its protective coverings and is buried again in the earth against a future day. As each child spades in some soil, they remind each other that this is hallowed ground. They are being obedient to God's commandment to be a record-keeping people.

For this family, the reality of the Book of Mormon's origin is unquestioned. They've not only been taught the details and unique missions of Moroni and Joseph Smith, but they have also experienced making records and preserving them.

Pictures are valuable records too, particularly if they are appropriately identified.

One morning several years ago I arose while the house was still quiet to go downstairs to start dinner preparations. It was Mother's Day and mother had to get with it. There on the floor in front of the door to our bedroom was a treasured gift. It was a three-by-seven-foot collage of our family from the first child to the present time. Our eldest daughter had spent more than two hundred hours enlarging hundreds of old snapshots and new negatives so that family figures varied in size. Then with her artist's skill she cut, glued, and varnished our history as a family.

Dinner preparations were considerably delayed. I sat down and studied this magnificent "other kind of record" and wept. And wept. I sighed and marveled. I laughed as I looked at it again and again. The amazing effort I appreciated, of course. Our daughter's talents were thoroughly familiar to me. She was a professional. But it was overwhelming for me to see there before my eyes the sweep of the years. There were all my homes. There were my babies, my first-day-of-schoolers, my mischief makers, my Halloween spooks, my Nativity people, my teen queens, my Eagle Scout, my missionary, my brides, my grandchildren. I say "my" because it was Mother's Day. I was grabbing my glory in the silence of the dawn. How can a parent ever express appreciation enough for such a gift?

Then I awakened my husband and we wept and laughed together, sharing this unique offering. It was our life.

Carla has since been commissioned to do this for other families who have seen ours. When our young daughter-in-law died an untimely death, Carla caught the essence of Christine by collaging her pictures, large and small, sad and glad, infant and girl, costumed and ball-ready, girl graduate and bride. What she had of life and what she was from infancy to young motherhood flows before us now. Words defy the description of this record's beauty and comfort in the lives of her loved ones.

A collage, pictures framed on a wall, pictures protected in an album, in slides, or on movie film are valuable records. But they should be clearly identified with an attached, written description of dates, places, occasion, and complete names, perhaps even relationships. Everyone has had the experience of wondering who in the world certain people are in a picture!

Pictures, letters, and other kinds of records besides journal and genealogical sheets keep, always before our eyes, the traditions of our precious past — recent and long since — of the people with whom we have crossed paths, of the particular ones whom we have loved and become related to.

Are these some ideas for other kinds of record keeping that might work for your family?

We can't do much about the records that are handed to us or that we search about for, except preserve them. But we do have control over the records that we will turn over to others.

They speak for us — like the proverbial voices from the dust.

Writing a life story is singularly sweet and satisfying. How it all floods back! No wonder we cannot write the smallest part of what we feel. One musical bar may not be as moving as the concerto, nor a quote as inspiring as the sermon; still, in record keeping, a small effort is better than none. It permits us the sacrament of gratefulness.

The records we keep may find us somewhat in the position of Goethe, who said that in such matters he could promise to be sincere but not impartial. But keep them we must. Even if no one else ever reads them, the act of writing is its own reward.

Sources for our effort are near at hand. Our heart will help us. So will pictures stashed here and there, treasures on a tabletop, trivia in a small box, memorabilia of lifestyles past and present cluttering a dresser drawer, a pair of shoes — disreputable but indispensible, yearbooks, letters, certificates and cards, a well-worn, note-stuffed triple combination. And much else.

There are many kinds of materials that speak of a person's life. There are many methods of gathering them together in an orderly fashion.

Colorful people often write their memoirs, which is a kind of narrative of experiences that the writer has lived through. How much is fact and how much is narrative is seldom really known by anybody, including the writer. Objectivity, let alone truth, seems quite impossible. The value of such records may end with the writing.

Many great characters in history have published their autobiographies. This is the story of a person's life written by himself. It is one of the popular literary forms of our time. An autobiography is generally considered to be a more serious work than a memoir.

Genealogy is a record or table of the descent of a family, a group, or an individual from an ancestor or ancestors. It is a person's lineage. It is a pedigree or family tree. It usually includes facts and figures, dates and places, as well as name and relationship information. We are to have our genealogy and endowment records completed accurately as far back on each branch as is possible and ultimately have the temple work done for them, too. Continual research uncovers more and more information, encourages increasingly accurate records, and draws us all ever closer.

A personal record, journal, or diary is an account kept regularly of current happenings in one's life as well as feelings on life, the gospel, people, and so forth. We should all be keeping a current record of our life.

A life story is a record we write by looking back upon the past. Our task is to present ourselves, our gifts, our tendencies in relation to the circumstances of our time.

A personal history is a collection of genealogies, diaries or journals, if any, and a formal statement about one's life or a life story. It includes who we are, where we came from, and what we've been doing, so far, while we're here.

How to put life in a life story is the purpose of this book, though stimulating an interest in keeping a record of some kind should be considered a primary concern as well. We want to be able to pass down to our loved ones a personal record "worthy of all acceptation," as suggested in Doctrine and Covenants 128:24.

There are several systems for preparing a worthwhile and delightful personal history. One way is to live this kind of life. Another is to be creative and thoughtful, sensitive and sensible about what we record.

It usually helps, in the beginning at least, to have a theme or a format around which to build our life. This is a literary device, a thrust, a hook upon which to hang our history. Here are some possibilities:

Anecdotes. Telling a story through the means of anecdotes is easy reading for posterity. The incidents related should represent the stages of life. They can be humorous, spiritual, sentimental, or character-building, and they ought to be essentially true. They should involve us personally or some special friend or relative close enough to us so that our own life is revealed.

Attitudes. All through life we act and react according to our attitude about what happens to us. We can describe those events that changed our attitudes, tempered our behavior, or strengthened our beliefs. It would be a most helpful kind of life story. So much of what we'll write will depend upon how we look at our life, too. We can say nothing happened of interest to anyone else, so why write?

Or we can say everything happened to us, so why not write about it—whether anyone else might be interested or not?

Adventures. If we see life as a grand adventure, a school of preparation for heaven, we can choose for our history personal information and details that support this view. Adventure of conversion. The adventure of being a missionary. The adventure of being hospitalized. The adventure in working on a tugboat for the summer. The adventure of a survival course or family pack trip. The adventure in searching out family tombstones in the cemetery. Truth is still better than fiction. Title it an adventure, tell it as it is, and the reader will be convinced it is one of the most fabulous lives ever. And remember, the first reader will be the writer!

People. We can wrap a personal history around people we've crossed paths with who have helped us, influenced us, caused us pain, inspired us, taught us precious principles. Extended family members (in-laws, cousins, etc.), co-church workers, office help, the landlady, or neighbors are incredibly interesting, especially when we record our interaction with them. This is a fine method for telling a life story for those of us to whom people are really important.

Places. We can tell a life story by putting it in the sequences of where we have lived. Each address contains the happenings and personal growth for that period. Or the places can be the trips we've taken, including the one from heaven to our mother's arms first time around.

Principles. The eternal truths of the gospel could form the basis for building our life story. How did we learn to pray? How did we come to know God? What were the incidents that drove home honesty, virtue, and faith? Remember Enos's dramatic repentance? Our own struggles in life can be helpful to others someday as well, if they are recorded according to the Lord's principles for us to live by.

Facts. Some people understand the power of understatement. They are fact oriented. A writing style of this kind reveals much about the person. Such a soul might record, "Mother and I married December 15, 1891. Were happy all of our days." What that lacks in imagination, it makes up for in comfortable candor. A chronological account of the occurrences of one's life is an orderly way to get everything in, but some expression or testimony of personal feeling probably ought to accompany it.

Feelings. A sensitive, deeply spiritual person would have success writing a life story around the feelings of his heart over the years. The tender times, the romantic times, the learning times, the times in the lap of the Lord, the times prayers were answered, the times shame was endured, the times a family love swelled full, the time of conversion to good and sacred things.

69

Blessings. A personal history based on blessings and blessing counting would be impressive. Blessings or counsel given by us to our child and blessings received (including our patriarchal blessing) should be included in this system for a life record. What a lift to our spirits to write a life story through the process of blessing counting! What are we thankful for? If we start a list with a reason why, we'll be on our way to a full life's story before long.

Seasons. We can get a start on writing our life story by describing the Christmases we remember. Or perhaps it will be the family's vacation to the lake that will be the device to tell details of our life. I chose summer to start mine. I built my childhood on the lessons I learned when there was time enough. It started with an early recollection the summer I turned three and ended with the ending of the summer of my life — when I became a grandmother. Or we can do it by moving our life along from birthday to birthday, or one birthday out of each decade.

Spiritual Experiences. This category should be included in whatever format we decide upon. Sharing our spiritual experiences on paper is sure to benefit some descendant. And before we insist we haven't had a miracle in our life to write about, we might think in terms of blessing babies, being set apart as a priesthood leader, being asked to pray in sacrament meeting for the first time, going on a temple excursion to do baptisms for the dead, a door opened in answer to prayer about genealogical lines, the miracle of money needed for a mission, feeling the warm glow of witness burn within us when we, or someone we were listening to, bore testimony of Jesus Christ. Even one or two such references wrapped around the facts of birth and schooling will make a meaningful life story.

A life story, after all, should be just that, a life story. It should include the details and dates of births and deaths vital to us. It should list and describe family members, environment, education and professional accomplishments, church and community service, household affairs, and a proceeding of our days. Beyond this, our story coupled with genealogical records and sacred certificates becomes a fine personal history — and an act of obedience.

The first line we write can be significant. As we start a new record book or begin preparing a life story, having a good beginning promises a better body content. We should try to write an opening statement that makes the reader want to go on reading — something that will put a little life into the life story at once.

In the Church archives is a rare little volume, still unpublished and largely sheltered from the public eye. It is the personal journal of the Prophet Joseph Smith. I am a journal keeper and I wept when I examined his. The cover is dark and much handled. Inside is this inscription in the Prophet's handwriting: "Book bought on 29th November 1832 for the purpose to keep a minute account of all things that come under my observation and etc."

It is interesting to note that the purchase came two days after the revelation the Lord gave through Joseph regarding record keeping. The Prophet was among the first to follow the word of God, who counseled that records should be kept of church business and also "their manner of life, their faith, and works. . . ." (D&C 85:2.)

The first entry in the Prophet Joseph's personal diary reads, "Oh God, bless thou thy servant Joseph Smith." His first words were a prayer! If that were all we had of Joseph's personal writings, we'd know enough about him to be impressed. We'd know him to be a humble leader.

Wilford Woodruff's journal for 1864 opens this way: "I have lived to see 56 new years, and I have kept a daily journal of my life for the last 35 years. In some measure it is also a life of others. I have written many sermons and teachings of the Prophets Joseph Smith and Brigham Young and sermons of apostles and elders of the church. I have watched the signs of the times for many years and noted the fulfillment of prophecy."

Nephi took up his plates of sheeted metal and his writing instrument, then began the records that were "the proceedings of his days." His first line reads, "I, Nephi, having been born of goodly parents. . . ." At once we know this man honored his earthly parents.

The first line we write can be significant, intriguing,

coaxing. A portion of President Spencer W. Kimball's personal history has been published under the title *One Silent Sleepless Night*. His first line is an explanation that lures the reader into the rest of the writing. He is a poet as well as a prophet, our President Kimball. He writes, "This is a record of one silent, sleepless night which I spent in 1957 in a bedroom on the third floor of the Mission Home in New York City following major surgery in which I lost one vocal cord and part of another and then had staph infection following the surgery. For all the long hours of the seemingly endless night I suffered and reminisced...." This record is a beautiful retreat from bitter pain. It also introduces another writing style for the personal record keeper, a wonderful weaving of a current experience with recollections from childhood.

The following excerpt from President Kimball's record reveals what a workable format this is.

"The night is wearing on. The New Yorkers about us on Park and Fifth Avenues in their tuxedos and evening dresses are still early in their evening's festivities.

"I am wandering again, back to childhood. We are at a picnic, all the good Thatcher folks. We have come on horseback, in buggies and in wagons to old Cluff's ranch. We enjoy the great swings from the monumental cottonwoods. There is lemonade for sale. The picnic dinner is incomparable.

"The swim in the pond is the ultimate — everybody goes in swimming. No skimpy bathing suits here — people are wearing dresses, stockings, and overalls. Father is such a good swimmer. How I wish I could swim as he does! All over the great pond he moves easily and seemingly without effort. Now he comes for me, his little boy. I am on his back with my arms around his neck so tightly that he must constantly warn me. The water is deep and I am scared, and I plead with him to take me back to the shallow water. At last we feel ground, and I say, 'I'm all right now, Pa,' and I see him turn and swim off toward deep water. I start toward shore and step into a deep hole. Down, down, down! Water is filling my lungs.... I cannot scream! Why doesn't someone get help? Will they never rescue me? Someone has now seen my predicament. Pa has heard their screams and is after me. I am full of water and coughing, spitting, crying for a long time. I thought I was drowned.

"But how did I get way down to Arizona again? O yes, I heard the whistle of a boat on the East River, which reminded me of the youngsters swimming in it and diving from the scraggy rocks. We saw them last week as we took the Circle trip around Manhattan Island. How I wish I could swim like those little urchins! If I could have swum like that when I was a child — " (Bookcraft, 1975, pp. 23-26.)

Charles Lindbergh used this same method to record his own life story. It is most compelling. It reveals the boy that was as well as the man that came to be, and the answers to a life shine through in a charming way. It may well be a method that would work for other life-story enthusiasts:

"The fog doesn't pass. I go on and on through its white blankness. I'm growing accustomed to blind flying. I've done almost as much on this single trip as on all my flights before put together. Survival no longer requires such alertness. Minutes mass into a quarter-hour. A quarter becomes a half; then three-quarters. Still the waves don't appear. I'm flying automatically again through eyes which register but do not see —

" 'No! No, I can't lie down and sleep! No! No, I can't get out and walk. Rub your eyes, shake your head. You're over the middle of an ocean!'

"But I'm not over the middle of an ocean. I'm not in an airplane flying through the sky. I'm —

" 'CHARLES!'

"I hardly hear my nurse's voice above my heartbeat. I've slipped away from her guard to stare fearfully around the gray barn's corner.

" 'CHARLES, COME BACK!'

"A huge column of smoke is rising from our house, spreading out, and blackening the sky. Then that's what the shouts and noise all meant. That's why I was jerked away from my play so roughly and rushed down the kitchen steps. Our house is burning down!

" 'CHARLES!'

"A hand grasps my arm and pulls me behind the barn. 'Charles, you musn't watch!' My nurse is excited. She thinks it's too terrible for me to see. Where is my father — my mother — What will happen to my toys? —

" 'Right rudder, five degrees.'

" 'Father will build us a new house.'

"I hold Mother's hand tightly while she speaks, looking down on the still smoking ruins. It's the next day. Our entire house has sunk into the stone walls of its basement. I recognize our cookstove, under pipes beside the furnace. Next to it are twisted bedsteads. There's the hot-water boiler. There's the laundry sink. Everything is covered with the gray snow of ashes. Right at my feet is a melted, green-glass lump that was once a windowpane. Out of the pit, smoke-smutted but sharp-cut against thick leaves and sky, rises our brick chimney, tall and spindly without a house around it. And on the chimney mantelpiece, midway up its height, where the big living room once ended, is Mother's Mexican idol — a small, red-clay figure — the only object to pass undamaged through the fire. Of course some clothes and books were saved, and the men carried out a few pieces of furniture. But my toys, and the big stairs, and my room above the river, are gone forever —

" 'The compass needle is leaning again, I must swing the nose right with my rudder.' " (*Spirit of St. Louis*, p. 372.)

Recently I suggested to a friend that he take time to record an experience his aged father had had with the president of the Church. He was thoughtful as he listened to my answer to his question, "Why should I?" Finally, he commented on his reluctance to record anything. He spoke of the several volumes about his grandfather that gathered dust on the bookshelves. "I've never been able to make myself get interested in them. And he was a great man. Why should anyone get interested in what I record?"

I couldn't promise him anyone would. But I could assure him of a great time for himself once he got going. I also reminded him that the personal records in the Book of Mormon weren't read by anyone for many centuries but they are being read now.

I was sympathetic though. For many long years I've had a little volume on my bookshelf that I had seldom noticed, let alone read. It was written by my great-great-grandfather, Major Howard Egan, a pioneer pony express rider. The more older family members urged me to read this, the more I resisted. Then, with an interest in helping others keep personal records, I thumbed through the pages, stopped, went back to the beginning, and read with ever-increasing thoughtfulness and pleasure. I *know* one of my ancestors now. I know he was an avid record keeper. I know he was a good writer. I suspect that it might be from him I inherited my desire to write. I'm sure I'll look forward to a good visit with him someday. We'll have something in common. And I had thought he was "just another pioneer."

Names of people I've heard of, such as Heber C. Kimball and Brigham Young, Brother Olayton, and descriptions of people I haven't heard of, spill through his personal entries as he tells of experiences with them crossing the plains, fighting the Indians, settling the valley, and moving later parties from Winter Quarters west. He includes rules they lived by, inventories and personnel assignments. It is an education in pioneer life. It is also great reading. And the quality of character in my ancestor is evident. That warms me, and my heart turns to my fathers, just as the scriptures promise. This 1847 record proves how important the personal journal of ordinary people can be to others. Here is one excerpt:

"Tuesday, April 16th. — This morning the wind was north and it was cloudy. Brothers Little, Rockwood and Redding went to Winter Quarters to bring on Brother Little's things. At 7:30 the brethren were called together in order to organize them. The meeting was opened by prayer by President Young, after which G.A. Smith made some remarks; also H.C. Kimball, N.K. Whitney and others. The camp was divided into two divisions, 72 in each division; A.P. Rockwood captain of the First and S. Markham of the Second Division. Night guard was started and on the 17th the camp was organized under regiment. On the 18th the Council of Captains made laws regulating the camp as follows:

LAWS OR RULES.

"1. — After this date the horn or bugle shall be blown every morning at 5 a.m., when every man is expected to arise and pray; then attend to his team, get breakfast and have everything finished so that the camp may start by 7 o'clock.

"2. — Each extra man is to travel on the off side of the team with his gun on his shoulder, loaded, and each driver have his gun so placed that he can lay hold of it at a moment's warning.

"Every man must have a piece of leather over the nipple of his gun, or if it is a flintlock, in the pan, having caps and powder-flask ready.

"3.— The brethren will halt for an hour about noon, and they must have their dinner ready cooked so as not to detain the camp for cooking.

"4. — When the camp halts for the night, wagons are to be drawn in a circle, and the horses to be all secured inside the circle when necessary.

"5. — The horn will blow at 8:30 p.m., when every man must return to his wagon and pray, except the night guard, and be in bed by 9 o'clock, at which time all fires must be put out.

"6. — The camp is to travel in close order, and no man to leave the camp twenty rods without orders from the Captain.

"7. — Every man is to put as much interest in taking care of his brother's cattle, in preserving them, as he would his own, and no man will be indulged in idleness.

"8. — Every man is to have his gun and pistol in perfect order.

"9. — Let all start and keep together, and let the cannon bring up the rear, and the company guard to attend it, traveling along with the gun, and see that nothing is left behind at each stopping place."

We could list the rules our families live by. Revealing! Have you ever thought about including an inventory of personal belongings? My great-grandfather did, as well as one of the camp supplies. There is a story in a list of commodities with the value estimated, too.

Everybody enjoys a good story. So, of course, the more life we put into our life story, the more pleasurable it will be as a record for both reader and writer. All that means is that we should be well buckets coming up full when we look at our own life. Our enthusiasm and gratefulness will carry over into the record.

I love the incident a relative of mine shared when his son was filling a mission. He received a letter one week that began "Dear Dad, You are about to be given another blessing — I need more money!" The boy could have phrased it as a burden, a nuisance, or with an apology. That elder's attitude was positive and so was the father's response. I know a woman who never had any problems. She only had challenges, but plenty of those. Such a life story reflecting this kind of attitude would be lifting to any who came upon it in any generation.

Another aspect of record keeping is to train our children to keep records. This, as in other valuable behavior, must be instilled in them in the earliest years. Of course, they'll learn from our enthusiasm for record keeping and from our example in actually doing it. But watching and hearing are no match for actually experiencing the satisfaction of record writing and preserving and respecting inherited documents. We need to look for opportunities to get them involved in some phase of record keeping.

When our six were little their father was called to be a bishop again. We already knew about long and tiresome Sunday afternoons for those of us at home. Then we began using the time for record keeping. After dinner, each child was wrapped in one of my aprons to protect Sunday-best clothing as we sat around the table and lost ourselves in our heritage. Most of them couldn't read or write yet, but what they lacked in these skills they made up for in enthusiasm. Sunday soon became their favorite day.

Each child had a personal book of remembrance. Everything was copied six times over — pictures for the pedigree charts, life stories, and family group sheets. Most of them had come from the hospital to a different home, and each had been blessed in a different chapel. There were pictures of these places to gather, scenes of family holidays, and "grand occasions" to glue into place. And while the scissors and paste pot passed from one little hand to another and back, we spun stories from what little I knew about their ancestors, and conjectured what each child's contribution might be. We even went so far as to give credit for physical features and talents one or the other of them might have inherited from this or that ancestor. It was a marvelous mess and they loved it. The books may not have survived the bishop's term of duty, yet they gave the children roots for their future branching tree. They became generation-interested and record-keeping oriented at this impressionable age. They're grown up and on their own now but they all keep records.

My husband's grandfather, President George Q. Cannon, felt strongly about record keeping. He had three records that he kept concurrently. One was a personal journal of his activities, one contained information from meetings of the First Presidency of the Church, and the third was a private diary of his inner feelings and spiritual growth. He had accounts of his travels as well. These journals are treasures for what they reveal about the times, the Church, personalities, and the character traits of a remarkable man.

Often President Cannon used his own sons as secretaries or scribes for these records so they would be drawn close to him, have a responsibility in life, and learn how to make proper entries in a journal. When Clawson Y. Cannon was fifteen years old he accompanied his father, President Cannon, to Hawaii for the fiftieth anniversary of the establishment of the Church there. President Cannon had had a remarkable mission those many years before, so the journals of the return trip are interesting by comparison. But for our purposes here, it is the fact that he dictated the important happenings along the way to his fifteen-year-old son in a manner the boy could understand. This is one way to get your child to learn what you want him to learn and to get him to read your life story! Of course that boy Clawson would grow up to be a devoted Church member and an avid record keeper himself. Past ninety years of age, he still writes regularly in his journal.

The following unedited excerpt, dictated by President Cannon to his son, reveals the inspiration we can get from one man's personal journal whether we are related to him or not:

"I must say that there were two things which I dreaded very much upon leaving home, one was the sea voyage, the other was my inability to talk the native language. For 46 years had past since I left and I have done very little in talking the Hawaiian language since that time. The sea voyage through the blessing of the Lord and prayers of the Brethren was a most pleasant one and furnished no cause for dread, the language also through the favor of the Lord came to me in a manner to surprise me. When I was called upon this morning to speak I did so principally in English and spoke with great power. The spirit rested powerfully upon me but while preaching in English the spirit of the Lord would bring the native Language back to me and I would break out in it to the surprise of my self and the delight of the people for it was a great cause of wonder to them that I should be able to speak in their language at all after so long an absence from the Islands. I was made to feel very happy through this blessing of the Lord upon me for He removed all my causes for dread. It was so every time I spoke during the two days of the celebration."

And then this sacred entry, which could not help but impress the scribe as well as any reader: "I wanted to find if possible where Nalinanui lived when she gave us shelter . . . . and the garden where I sought the Lord in secret prayer and where he condescended to commune with me for I heard his voice more than once as one man speaks with another encouraging me and showing to me the work which should be done among this people if I would follow the dictates of his spirit. Glory to God in the highest that he has permitted me to live to behold the fulfillment of his words."

The style is simple so the boy could properly record it. The spelling and sentence structure are touchingly imperfect in the unedited journal typical of his own age. But the spirit comes through. Such a testimony calls forth our own. It is good the journal was kept.

Incidentally, though the imperfect speller grew up to be a brilliant, highly educated university professor and department head, this record made during his youth is the more precious, more personally revealing because of its mistakes.

Even the person who feels uneducated should not be reluctant to record his feelings and experiences. The blessings of the Lord come to us in many settings. They'll touch our hearts in the reading whether the spelling is correct or the literary style is professional or not.

As we learn in the Book of Mormon, the Lord can make weakness in writing strength in the reading.

Sometimes a personal journal can reveal a lesson the Lord wants the reader to learn. Such a thing occurred when a young woman of our day read a journal entry made by Zina D. H. Young years ago regarding the gift of tongues. Though the spiritual gift was different in the two instances, Sister Young's experience heartened the young woman to accept her own spiritual gifts appropriately. Again, a personal record has value for one who is not even related to the writer of the record.

Zina D. H. Young had been baptized and confirmed by

Hyrum Smith when she was a young girl. "Soon after," writes Sister Young in her journal, "the gift of tongues rested upon me with overwhelming force. I was somewhat alarmed at this strange manifestation, and so checked its utterance. What was my alarm, however, to discover that upon this action upon my part, the gift left me entirely, and I felt that I had offended that Holy Spirit by whose influence I had been so richly blessed. I suffered a great deal in my feelings over the matter, and one day while mother and I were spinning together, I took courage and told her of the gift I had once possessed and how, by checking it I had lost it entirely.

"Mother appreciated my feelings, and told me to make it a matter of earnest prayer, that the gift might once more be given to me. I walked down to a little spring in one of the meadows, and as I walked along I mused on my blessing and how I had turned away the spirit of God. When I reached the spring I knelt down and offered up a prayer to God and told him if he could forgive my transgression and give me back the lost gift I would promise never to check it again, no matter where or when I felt its promptings.

"I have kept this vow, but it has been a cross at times, for I know that this gift is the least of all gifts, and it is oftentimes misunderstood and even treated lightly by those who should know better. Yet it is a gift of God, and should not be despised by him who receives it, but magnified to the extent, even as the lowest grade of the priesthood is the least of all, and yet it needs be magnified as earnestly as are the higher and great offices!"

This is a single incident in the life of a girl. Though it may make us want to know more about her life story, it is a satisfying sample. One needs only to remember the incident with the basin to know Christ was a masterful master. Still, the details of his resurrection give us witness of his divinity. What a crime to mankind if only the basic incident had been recorded. We do not need to know the daily log of activities, the color of all one's clothing, to get the picture of the soul, but the incidents we choose to write will be important.

With this in mind, for our own life story we should write enough to let people become aware of our growth and progress in life but not so much as to bore them into not reading further. Perfection is a process, not a state of being

— for us in the world, at least. A life story should be inclusive of sufficient incidents to reflect the writer to the reader.

In writing a life story and keeping a personal journal we need to reach the happy medium between the colorless, meaningless platitudes or the full rehearsal of hourly duties and the verbose, never-ending recitations of trials, tribulations, and ecstasies.

A life story written after the fact is something we have control of and can use literary discipline with more than we can in a journal with its entries made along life's way. However, care should be used in journal keeping, too. Few have time enough to wade through volumes and volumes of scrawling handwriting. Written for personal therapy, such entries no doubt have value. But if we hope to influence posterity, restraint must be used or posterity will never read a word.

There are two things to remember about record keeping, then; one is to do it, and the other is to try to do it in as fine a fashion as possible. The first is certainly more important than the latter, but once begun, our interest in improving the quality of it will sharpen. There are many fine helps available short of a college course in expository writing. For those of us who have to put words on paper (and surely that must be the whole human race!) the classic one is Strunk and White's little paperback *The Elements of Style*. It has been around a long time, revised several times. It still works in giving understandable instruction on how to put words together, when to leave words out, what a good sentence is, proper grammar and punctuation. It includes fine examples of what is and is not an interesting bit of writing.

Our purpose here is not to go into all of that, though we heartily recommend the pursuit. Rather, we hope to encourage everyone, skilled writer and untrained soul, to record the facts and the color of his or her life — and to do it with a little care and flare.

There used to be a bit of philosophy I conjured up for myself to live by that worked for me. I'd remind myself that painful things are to be tucked away in my mind to draw strength and direction from in future times of trial. But the sweet things — ah, the sweet things are to be tucked away in my heart to cherish. And to bask in.

I was very young then.

It all seemed so simple.

Fortunately I didn't depend entirely on my mind or my heart. I kept a diary.

At first my record keeping was accomplished in a five-year diary with lock and key. And I hid the key. Then I graduated to a one-year version in my early teens. I had a lot more to write by then. I had made a vow to keep a diary so that when I grew up and worked in the Church I would understand how teenagers felt. I'd be a better youth leader that way. I don't recall exactly what experience generated this attitude, but I remember feeling strongly about it, and I made a record of it. It was the motivation for regular soul-searching entries for years.

During that period I religiously wrote down my feelings, my yearnings, my complaints, my parties and dates, the movies we saw, the lessons we had in church, whether the bishop greeted me or not, and all my observations of people old and young in their various situations.

Life was exciting to me then because I was so alive to it with my purpose of observing for the record.

I soon became annoyed by the barriers imposed by a dated book of any kind. I was keeping a daily entry but sometimes there was much more to record than at other times. Because I was an active Mutual Improvement Association maid, I turned to the cumbersome Treasures of Truth book in which to pour out my heart and my mind. Soon after, I shifted to the genealogical-width sheets so they'd fit in a book of remembrance. But that didn't seem the appropriate place for my kind of personal record keeping.

In later years I tried the big commercially issued journals, impressive in binding and boasting attached ribbon markers, like the scriptural records. They intimidated me. What did I have to write that was all that grand? And what if I didn't live so long and all those pages were left wasted? Besides, I needed something slender, to fill up quickly, to change with the season if need be and allow me plenty of fresh starts! It must be compact so it would travel, unimpressive so the children wouldn't want to snoop into it when they were little, but sturdy enough to be around when they were old enough to attach proper value to mother's journals.

Now, our clever bookbinding daughter Susan has provided me with the perfect answer. It is a gem. It meets my personal requirements and is satisfying to me aesthetically. She covers a standard 5″ x 8″ record book in a variety of lovely fabric, unusual paper, artwork, or a frieze of family pictures. These little books (several dozen of them by now) are valuable even without my entries. Perhaps this idea will help you.

Personally, I think record keeping is one of the special commandments from God. I am thankful beyond expression that I have kept a written record of some kind since I was a child. I am also thankful that as the years have lent their luster and lessons to my life, I have learned a good deal more about the value of this effort. This has affected my record keeping now. This change in style and content tells its own story.

I am appalled just how easy it is to forget the precious past, how impossible it seems at times to get proper perspective of an experience when the details of it have disappeared. The mind and heart have become crowded with so much of life. I understand that the older we get the harder it is for most of us to recall what happened yesterday, let alone some years ago.

There is another factor, too. Time sweeps the seasons so swiftly by. Keeping records now, when it is happening, is even more important for me today because my whole fifty years — give or take a few — seem to have passed in a weekend!

For example, I can no longer really remember uncataclysmic but oh-so-important things like which child it was who left the note under my pillow one night long ago that stirred me as I tried to sleep. It was so poignant at the time that I never worried about being able to take that moment out of my heart to bask in it when I wanted to. But so many children, so many notes later, whose was which? There is value in knowing for certain. Value for me, for the child, grown now, and for a descendant yet unborn, perhaps. Why, the note writer could be that person's grandparent! Fortunately I do have a written record of such moments in my life.

83

A record keeps the record straight. We make an entry but save the evidence, too. That is good record keeping.

Many of us have made the innocent mistake of foolishly saying, "I'll never forget . . ." as we reminisce with family and friends. Soon we learn we have, in fact, forgotten. Our spouse corrects us. Friends remind us of precious but forgotten details. A child insists upon the full truth. We do not remember all that we'd like to, even all that we ought to, and especially not all that we thought we would. A record of some kind is invaluable to trigger a full recollection of mood, faces, scent, aura, and implication.

To read back on the time my response to an inner impulse saved the life of a four-year-old we dearly loved is rewarding to me even now. It points up a "marking" in my spiritual development, too. It was an early witness to me that the Holy Ghost warns of danger, and one can be repeatedly thankful for any effort made to stay in tune. I would be grateful if someone were to read the account someday and be moved upon to seek after the Spirit.

Wilford Woodruff kept records that have become the prototype for personal journals in our time. They are informative and inspirational. They also contain valuable details unrecorded anywhere else. And they are a joy to read. President Woodruff wrote of not being able to sleep at night until he had recorded every word the Prophet Joseph Smith preached in his presence. He wrote of being blessed by the Spirit to have total recall of the expressions and sermons of the Prophet. We are indebted to these personal journals for a record of many of the Prophet's teachings, for fascinating life-style details of the day.

We may not be a Wilford Woodruff with such portentious things as a prophet's revelations to record, but we can write by the Spirit if we will seek after it and live worthily for it. If ever we do happen to be in a position to hear with our own ears one of the servants of the Lord, surely we should immediately record the experience and pray for guidance in doing so.

We lived in the same ward as President and Sister Harold B. Lee. I am grateful that I was in the congregation during fast and testimony meeting December 1974. Sister Lee was in her usual place and though President Lee was frequently on the stand, this particular day he hadn't been present. As a member of the bishopric closed the meeting, we heard the familiar voice of President Lee come from the back of the room where he had just joined us. He apologized for interrupting the meeting. Then he bore a most remarkable and spiritually strengthening witness of sacred things, addressed to us personally as his neighbors, beloved friends, members of his ward family, and the "flock" over whom he had stewardship. It was an unusually powerful and specific witness, and my heart pounded as he spoke.

This turned out to be the last ward testimony meeting of President Lee's life, for he died three weeks later, the day after Christmas. We couldn't know this when he stood among us that day. Had I waited to write about the experience until after his funeral, my perspective no doubt would have been different. But I went home and took time right then to write, praying as I did so.

Now this whole precious experience has meant more to me than to many there that day, I've learned, because I listened carefully as prompted by the Spirit and as a trained journalist. I went home and recorded it at once. I have taken occasion to reread the record to fill assignments to write about it for certain histories and to lift my spirits, too. It has meant more with each reading. Surely it will be valuable evidence some day for each one of my posterity to read of a prophet's powerful witness of the Savior.

For myself I cannot *not* write. I am a driven woman, powerless to withstand the lure of pen and pad. I respond easily to the promptings of what to write and when. I even write down precious happenings in the lives of others, and their bright sayings and inspired remarks as well, especially if I know they aren't record keepers — yet, keeping a personal journal and compiling a life history are not perfunctory, duty-bound actions for me. They are not considered part of my daily grind. Record keeping for me is a delight and privilege. It is, as I have said, a kind of compulsion. There have been times, of course, when I have had to make time for the task of record keeping. But I do it because I am an enthusiastic believer in the principle. I am not only compulsive, I am committed. For me, finding the time and the inclination to record in comfortable proximity is simply a matter of priorities. I have lived long enough now to know the real values in written memories.

After the scriptures, the records I hold most sacred are my own. And among my own records the writings I hold most valuable are my experiences with Heavenly Father and the Lord Jesus Christ. Then I treasure the written memory (recorded when fresh upon me) of certain special interactions with loved ones, with others, and with the awesome exigencies of life itself. I also hold sacred the other kinds of records one can inherit or gather along the way, such as a letter from our missionary, a written apology from a man far greater and more important that I, a patriarchal blessing so consistently referred to, a document of merit, a transcript of a devotional speech, a lesson manual I taught from or helped write, a published portion of my life story, a photo collage of our family, a memo of love from my husband, and one of comfort from my father on his letterhead when my girl-heart was breaking years ago. These and other kinds of records I have preserved because they might be of worth to others someday. But otherwise, I record in my journal what would be of value to me.

I've had one real traumatic experience with record keeping and disposing of evidence that might be helpful to the reader, however. I had earned my college keep as a columnist and reporter for the old Salt Lake *Tribune-Telegram.* Then for twenty-five years I was associated with the *Deseret News* as an editor and then a daily columnist. All that time I kept carbon copies of my efforts as well as clippings of the printed word — over 15,000 articles. There were all the other writings I saved evidence of, too. There were scripts, manuscripts, published and rejected, biographies, feature articles, national magazine assignments, and all my church writings over the years. When we sold our family home and changed our life-style, a decision had to be made about these great mounds of collections from only one portion of my past. A whole wall of my study had been especially built with file cases like bookshelves for these records, and I couldn't take it all with me.

One day in the packing process I weighed sentiment against sense — even against obedience. Sentiment lost. What were a few thousand columns when a family home was being wiped out? Besides, I wondered, who really cared? The past was past, I rationalized. It's vanity to keep such clutter, I lamented. I decided to burn the twenty-five-plus years of carbons and clippings.

But I did it with a flourish.

I built a fire at sunset in the charcoal pit and tossed clipping after carbon onto the coals.

I wept. Soft tears fell as the flames flared with my records. You see, most of this material had been written on a daily basis before the "dawn patrol" streetcar to college. Later they were written on a daily basis before the 6 a.m. feeding of each new baby, before the six a.m. Scout hike, the six a.m. pep club practice, and the six a.m. car pool for early-morning seminary. The rest had been written from my bed while in the hospital for deliveries, surgeries, and sympathy over the years. They had been written with one infant on my lap and other children competing for a typing turn.

They weren't just carbons and clippings after all. They were leaves from my life. They reflected the times of the community, to be sure, but they reflected, indirectly, the times of the Cannon household.

Of course I cried!

It may have been a rash mistake to burn all that record. I should have been selective, at least. My family thinks so.

The point is, in personal record keeping — writing or gathering things about our life and our family's history—we cannot write nor can we save everything. Selection, too, then becomes a part of records. Our Book of Mormon scribes taught us this. The critical counsel here is to *do it*. Write down, gather, save. When disposing of these materials is forced upon us, selection must be made on the basis of those things that are worthwhile, that persuade to do good and be good, that remind of the choice times, and that testify of God. These are the things to be held sacred, preserved, and passed on to the next generation.

We, like Mormon, may end up doing some abridging of our own records, if time and retirement permit. Surely we don't want to leave a legacy of pain. Nor will we want our records in such a state that they are regarded as trash after we are gone. It helps if there is a format or an order to the way a life is recorded. If it is a diary or journal we are keeping, we ought to put the month, day, and year with each entry. When I am away from home I add the city, details of my housing, and the company I'm keeping. It provides a setting for whatever entries follow.

Professional historians urge that records be kept on as high a quality, nonacid paper as possible to prevent deterioration. Also, we should use only black ink or black typewriter ribbon, so the copy can be picked up on copying machines. I've had the very real thrill of examining the original manuscripts of the Book of Mormon written by Oliver Cowdery as the Prophet Joseph Smith dictated during the translation process. Some of the writing now is barely visible, it has faded so in a hundred years. Many portions of the pages have dissolved completely with age. The remaining manuscript now has been protected and preserved in a handsome leather case. We should take precautions by using good materials in the first place and storing them under lock and key in a metal strong box or fireproof case of some kind.

All of this is a clear case for record writing and record preserving. If you haven't been much of a record keeper — sort of a modern-day Chemish — perhaps you'll become one now. If you do, every year you will be happier that you started when you did. I can testify to that. I ache over the gaps in my life's story, those prolonged periods of personal silence that circumstances forced upon me. And I wish I had started even sooner. You see, the crickets sing at noon for me, now. It is comforting to have recorded evidence of where the years went. It's like having money in the bank or food stored against the season. Only better. Record keeping is a task the body performs but the spirit thrives under.

One day (with our present being obediently recorded) perhaps we can program some time to get caught up on the past, writing the pertinent things we can recall from the yesterdays. When we prayerfully start this particular task, the Spirit will quicken us. We will remember. We will feel the affirmation from Heavenly Father that our obedience is pleasing to him. At least this has been so with me.

When Christ visited the Nephites in America nearly 2,000 years ago he said, "Bring forth the record which ye have kept." If such a call should come to us, we would want to be able to comply.

We, like Omni, may not keep all the commandments of the Lord. Still we can easily keep this perfectly delightful, personally satisfying one of writing down the meaningful moments in life.

"For we labor diligently to write, to persuade our children, and also our brethren, to believe in Christ, and to be reconciled to God; for we know that it is by grace that we are saved, after all we can do.

"And we talk of Christ, we rejoice in Christ, we preach of Christ, we prophesy of Christ, and we write according to our prophecies, that our children may know to what source they may look for a remission of their sins." (2 Nephi 25:23, 26.)

And death hath come upon our fathers; nevertheless we
know them. . . . For a book of remembrance we have written . . . and in our own language. (Moses 6:45-46.)